THE FOOTSTEPS OF

ANNE FRANK

by

ERNST SCHNABEL

Translated from the German by

RICHARD AND CLARA WINSTON

southbank
publishing

This edition published in 2014 by Southbank Publishing
PO Box 394, Harpenden, Herts, AL5 1XJ

www.southbankpublishing.com

Foreword by Erika Prins, Historian at the Anne Frank House, Amsterdam
© 2014 Anne Frank House Amsterdam
In writing the foreword Erika Prins used the following edition for reference,
Spur eines Kindes. Ein Bericht von Ernst Schnabel, Fischer Taschenbuch Verlag, 1987,
Frankfurt am Main

Sources for the quotes:
Letter of Otto Frank to Manfred George (*Aufbau*), Mai 12th 1957
Collection Anne Frank House, Amsterdam

Letter of Ernst Schnabel to Miep Gies, August 28th 1957,
Collection Anne Frank House, Amsterdam

Letter of Ernst Schnabel to Otto Frank, September 13th 1957,
heritage of Ernst Schnabel, at the Deutschen Literaturarchiv of the
Schiller-Nationalmuseum, Marbach am Neckar

Introduction by Gillian Walnes MBE,
Co founder and Executive Director, The Anne Frank Trust UK
©2014 Anne Frank Trust UK

A CIP catalogue record for this book is available from the British Library.

ISBN: 978-1-904915-38-6

2 4 6 8 10 9 7 5 3 1

Typeset by Avocet Typeset, Somerton, Somerset
Printed and bound by CPI Group (UK) Ltd, Croydon CR0 4YY

The Footsteps of Anne Frank

The name of Anne Frank is known throughout the world. The diary which this young girl wrote while for twenty-five months she and her family were hidden in the back part of an Amsterdam office building has made her a symbol of the millions of Jews who suffered and perished like her. Anne Frank died in the concentration camp at Belsen at the age of sixteen.

The story of Anne's life before the *Diary*'s start and of the tragedy that followed its abrupt ending has not hitherto been told. Ernst Schnabel has tracked down and interviewed almost every person now living who knew her. Anne's father, sole survivor of the family, is the first witness; more than forty others add their testimony. And Anne herself speaks too, in some of her unpublished writings.

The later sections of this book are almost unbearably poignant. They reveal that after the family's betrayal to the Gestapo and transportation to the concentration camp of Auschwitz, Anne's affectionate nature still showed itself in little acts of kindness to her companions; and even when she and her sister were taken from their parents and sent to die in the hell of Belsen her shining spirit remained indomitable to the last.

CONTENTS

Foreword by Erika Prins   9

Introduction by Gillian Walnes MBE   15

1   *The Focus and the Paths*   21

2   *The Beginning of the Trail and the Shadow*   27

3   *When We Were Still in Normal Life*   41

4   *Ten Seconds*   61

5   *Deadlines and Top-Secret Orders*   67

6   *The Walk in the Rain*   81

7   *Marginal Notes*   93

8   *More Deadlines*   119

9   *The Final Solution*   127

10   *Visiting Hours after 9am*   143

11   *The Journey into Night*   151

12   *The End of the Trail and the Moss*   169

13   *The Diary of Anne Frank*   183

FOREWORD

Spur eines Kindes by Ernst Schnabel (known in English as *The Footsteps of Anne Frank*) is a special book, a book with a history. Special because of its origins, because of the place that it occupies in the 'world of Anne Frank', because of its proximity in time to the events described, and not least, because of the emotional involvement of the author in the fate of Anne Frank. A book that 50 years after its first publication in German, and many reprints and numerous translations later, is now rightly available again, because it brings to life history through the words and perceptions of those who were directly involved.

Ernst Schnabel began his career as a writer in the years before World War II. During the war he served in the German navy, and afterwards found himself working for the Northwest German Broadcasting (NWDR) in Hamburg. This radio broadcaster was created by the military government in the British zone of occupation in Germany, and it had close ties with the BBC. Schnabel made a cultural programme for the NWDR, and gained experience at the BBC in London. Here he became familiar with a genre of radio documentary, the so-called radio feature: a subject is brought to life through a combination of reports, interviews, documentation and elements of the radio play, all in a dramatic setting. For Germany, this was something completely new, and in the early fifties Schnabel acquired a great reputation as a pioneer in the field. As chief dramatist and controller at the NWDR he made countless documentaries.

Das Tagebuch der Anne Frank (*The Diary of Anne Frank*), from the publisher Lambert Schneider, first appeared in Germany in November 1950, in an edition of 4,600 copies. The sales figures were disappointing and it took a long time for a second edition to appear.

The mid nineteen-fifties saw increasing worldwide interest in Anne Frank and her diary. This was the time when the stage adaptation by American writer couple Goodrich and Hackett was drawing full houses in America, and in the meantime Europe had had its own premiere of the play. Negotiations were also under way to perform the play in Germany. Around that time, in 1957, the Anne Frank House was established as an independent non-profit organisation so that the family's hiding place at 263 Prinsengracht in Amsterdam could be preserved.

Otto Frank considered the wide distribution of the diary among young Germans to be very important, but in his view that was only possible with a cheaper edition. He was right, for in March 1955 after the paperback of *The Diary of Anne Frank* was printed by Fischer Bücherei in an edition of 50,000 copies, 30,000 were sold within the first month. Then, with the arrival of the 375 thousandth copy of the paperback in the spring of 1957, the publisher suggested that Otto Frank provide a brief introduction to the book. The publisher had received many letters, and an increasing number of people wanted to know more about this girl, the author of the diary. Who was she, where did she come from? The Dutch and German editions differed from each other. That prompted questions. And not all the questioners appeared to be in good faith. During this period the first voices raising doubts about the authenticity of the diary were heard, and Otto Frank was determined to dispel these doubts. Eventually, in collaboration with Otto Frank, Dr. Fischer of the publishing house decided on approaching Ernst Schnabel – not for an introduction, but for a whole new book in the same paperback series. In 1955 Ernst Schnabel had already considered the idea of making a radio adaptation of *The Diary of Anne Frank*, and he had been in contact with Otto Frank. Frank had been very interested, but before the premiere of the play in Germany a radio adaptation was out of the question.

Fischer arranged a meeting in May 1957 with Otto Frank and Ernst Schnabel in Frankfurt am Main. They were quick to agree. Ernst Schnabel would write a book for Fischer Bücherei and also make a radio adaptation based on documents, interviews with people whom Anne Frank had known, and especially with Otto Frank himself. The final version would be subject to Otto Frank's approval. They had to act quickly, because the book was due for release in the spring of 1958. The German premiere of the play was scheduled for October 1, 1957. Otto Frank was fully behind the project and lost no time, as is shown by a letter written the day after the meeting in Frankfurt and sent to *Aufbau*, the leading German-Jewish immigrants' magazine in New York:

'Fischer Publishers is planning to create a book based on authentic information about Anne. I only came into contact with a few people that were together with my wife and my two daughters Margot and Anne in Birkenau-Auschwitz or Bergen-Belsen. Those that I spoke with briefly after the war, I've lost track of again. I would now like, through an announcement or small article in *Aufbau*, to ask anyone who was together with my family in the camps to get in contact with me. I leave it to your judgment, how best to proceed. Of course, I will pay for the cost of an advertisement or an article.'

In *The Footsteps of Anne Frank* and in the radio adaptation, the hand of the documentary maker is clearly recognisable.

The book reads like a radio report and Schnabel's notes for it convey real atmosphere. In a letter he wrote to Miep Gies in 1957 about this:

'I need living people. Otherwise the result will be a dead thing. And I need also living, tangible people so that the reader can feel that Anne was living among real people and not among paper witnesses.'

Ernst Schnabel followed the 'trace' of Anne Frank and interviewed a large number of people who had consciously or unconsciously crossed her path. In the spring of 1957 Ernst Schnabel was in Amsterdam, and he literally followed her footsteps: to school, to her favourite ice cream shop, and around the neighbourhood she described in her diary. He made several visits to the hiding place, talked in particular with Otto Frank, and together with him visited friends, teachers and other acquaintances of Anne. Schnabel also spoke with Dr. Lou de Jong, director of the Institute for War Documentation created after the war in the Netherlands, and did his own research there. During his time in Amsterdam, Schnabel met several times with George Stevens, who at that time was working on shooting the Hollywood film version of the diary for Twentieth Century Fox. After Amsterdam he visited Bergen-Belsen, Frankfurt am Main and met once again with Otto Frank and his second wife in Switzerland. In early July 1957 Schnabel had finished his research and he set himself to writing. Based on the data gathered from his witnesses, on documents and his own observations he created *The Footsteps of Anne Frank*, a personal, passionate portrait of Anne Frank.

As agreed Schnabel presented the manuscript to Otto Frank. Miep and Jan Gies, Bep Voskuijl, Johannes Kleiman,

Victor Kugler (faithful helpers while in hiding) and Charlotte Kaletta (widow of the dentist Pfeffer) and Dr. Lou de Jong also got to read the manuscript. They all gave very precise comments to Schnabel, most of which he took into account. He acted upon their comments meticulously, and with integrity. Whilst he was working on the book he always kept in mind – as he had written to Otto Frank – what Dr. Rudolph Hirsch at the publishing house had told him: 'Do not under any circumstances, disturb the legend that is forming.' And that is why he chose to let the trail of Anne dissolve in Bergen-Belsen.

But for Schnabel this legend had to be truthful and he did not want to give the story an end, a 'death certificate' based on someone's dubious testimony about the last moments of Anne. At that time he had to take care in how he told Anne Frank's story, to avoid being met with disbelief and hostility. Schnabel wanted to stir awareness and empathy and gradually a willingness amongst people to accept responsibility for what had happened to Anne Frank and the millions of Jews under Hitler.

Schnabel was not a historian or scientist, but a writer and radio producer. He let the witnesses speak, and this is precisely the characteristic of the book.

In the vast sea of publications about her that have appeared since *The Footsteps of Anne Frank*, the memories of those interviewed have often been accepted as established fact, and repeated again and again. It is obvious that in the past 50 years, some of these recollections have been overtaken by historical research, and also many new facts have been discovered. But despite this aspect, the book remains of great value, because of the integrity of the author, his connection with his subject and the fact that he was close to the historical events. He heard everything first hand. The overwhelming awareness of Anne Frank was still new. On his visit to Bergen-Belsen, he saw the remains of the barracks burned by the British to prevent the spread of infectious diseases after the liberation of the camp. He made several visits to the hiding place on the Prinsengracht, then not yet a museum, and only recently saved from demolition. The pictures on the walls of Anne's room were taken to safety by Otto Frank, the hinges of the bookcase hung loose. On the floor of Anne's room, he saw a bunch of flowers, left by one of the first visitors – visitors who increasingly sought out the former hiding place on their own.

The Footsteps of Anne Frank has had many editions, and been translated into 21 languages. Surprisingly there has never been a complete edition in Dutch. This was at the express request of the helpers. They did not want their real names to appear in the book. They understood the importance of the book for Otto Frank and therefore granted it their full cooperation, but they did not want to be known themselves. The radio adaptation was not allowed to be broadcast in the Netherlands, either. The helpers felt that they had 'just' done their duty, and for them the tragic outcome was still too fresh in the memory.

For the radio broadcast of *The Footsteps of Anne Frank*, Ernst Schnabel received in 1958, the Prix des droits de l'Homme at the Prix Italia, and in 1959 the Heinrich Stahl Prize from the Jewish Community of Berlin.

Erika Prins,
historian, Anne Frank House (2014)

INTRODUCTION

Seven decades have passed since the end of World War 2 and over five decades since this book was written and published. This work, a mission conducted with great intensity and compassion, leaves footsteps of its own, the sense of loss described so emotively in the sublime writing, compounded by the loss over the ensuing years of those who bear witness within its pages. Many of the people you meet in the pages are now themselves the ghosts, just as Anne Frank was when Ernst Schnabel went on his mission to interview them.

I never met Anne Frank's father, as he died in 1980, but he has been a huge part of my own life. It was Otto Frank's wish to see an educational organisation in Britain in memory of his beloved daughter that subsequently brought about the Anne Frank Trust UK.

I have spoken about Otto Frank in many public speeches over the past quarter of a century, and often describe him as the polar opposite of, and counterbalance to, Adolf Hitler. Both men were born in 1889 and both fought as young men in the catastrophic Great War, and both men were proof that a single person can become an influencer of millions. One went on to wreak devastation and loss throughout Europe while the other went on to promote his daughter's writing as a force for good.

I was privileged however to spend time during the 1990s with Miep Gies, the courageous woman who helped the Frank family in hiding, and just before his death in 1993, her equally valiant husband Jan. I visited Miep a few times in her flat in Amsterdam. Once she took from a drawer the shopping list Herman van Pels had written for her to shop for the hiders' menial supplies, and a typed "menu" Anne's fertile imagination had created to mark Miep and Jan's first wedding anniversary. Together with Miep I attended the 1996 Academy Awards ceremony in Los Angeles, where Jon Blair's remarkable film "Anne Frank Remembered" won the Oscar that year for Best Documentary Feature. As an elderly white-haired woman mounted the stage to the audience's curiosity, Jon Blair told them and the millions watching on TV screens around the world, *"From a city of celluloid heroes, please meet a real one"*.

In her final years Miep still gave whatever she could of herself to ensure young people learned of the story of Anne Frank.

Not only are many of the people within these pages gone, but also the great chestnut tree which Anne wrote about and which Ernst Schnabel evokes. It is standing no more, blown down in a storm in 2009. Cuttings from it are planted in significant sites around the world.

This book was written in such different times, just 12 years after the liberation from Nazi tyranny and Anne's terrible tortured death of starvation and typhus in Bergen-Belsen. Schnabel hints at, but never explains, why he, as a German, felt so profoundly about what his own countrymen had perpetrated. At the time of writing the greatest threat seen to the Western world was that of Communism, the saccharine and "of its era" 1960 film "The Diary of Anne Frank" not yet released, although Miep refers to how she felt seeing the new stage play.

Schnabel describes visiting the empty hiding place to research his book and of "*the smell of mice and of ten years' silence and neglect*". The hiding place, which we now know as the Anne Frank House, currently receives over one million visitors a year. People from all over the globe line up patiently outside for a minimum of one hour, their patience rewarded with free Wifi while queuing.

We have a limited time now to speak to any of those who bore witness, which makes this book's reappearance after many years so important. At the Anne Frank Trust we work with thousands of young people a year who, when discovering what happened to this teenage girl, are shocked and angered into wanting to make the world better.

Anne Frank, through her life story and her words, through her personality and her contradictions, through her suffering and her ideals, challenges young people to try to make things better.

As educators we must continue to make what happened during those terrible times relevant, accessible and shocking to a generation of young people who are used to fast information and even faster answers. So many decades on, there must still be an electrical charge of outrage – like that which brought about the Universal Declaration of Human Rights three years after we saw into the gates of Auschwitz.

Gillian Walnes MBE,
Co-founder and Executive Director, Anne Frank Trust UK

AUTHOR'S NOTE

I wish to thank Director Dr L. de Jong and the Rijksinstituut voor Oorlogsdocumentatie, and Contact Publishers of Amsterdam, for their kindness in obtaining research material for me, and granting permission to reproduce this.

In addition to material supplied by the Rijksinstituut voor Oorlogsdocumentatie in Amsterdam, the following books were drawn upon for source material:

Dagboekfragmenten 1940–1945 (Martinus Nijhoff, The Hague, 1954).

The Final Solution, by Gerald Reitlinger (Vallentine, Mitchell & Co. Ltd., London, 1953).

The statements by Lies P. are based on newspaper accounts by Moshe Brilliant and M Y Ben-gavriêl.

The quotations from Anne Frank's writings other than those from her diary are published here for the first time.

For my children —
that they may know

CHAPTER 1

The Focus and the Paths

I have followed the trail of Anne Frank. It leads out of Germany and back into Germany, for there was no escape.

It is a delicate trail, winding to schools and through dreams, across the borders of exile to the threshold of her hiding place – and at the end becoming the pathway to death. It has been smudged by time and forgetfulness. In my search I followed up seventy-six persons who had known Anne and accompanied her some little distance, or had themselves gone similar ways, or who had knowingly or unknowingly crossed her path. Fifty of them were persons I found named or mentioned in Anne's diary. The names of others were given me in the course of my search or I ran across them by chance. Of these seventy-six persons, I found only forty-two. Eighteen were dead; only seven had died natural deaths. Ten others were either missing or, I was told, had left Europe. Six, I was unable to find at home. But forty-two persons have told me or written down for me what they remember of Anne. Some of them possess little mementos of her. There are photographs, brief pencilled greetings in the margins of letters from her parents, two swimming medals she won, a child's crib, a strip of film, an entry in a register of births and in a class roll, an outgrown wrap. There are, in short, small relics, little stories, and memories like wounds.

This book contains the testimony of my forty-two witnesses, as well as documents relating to the German occupation of the Netherlands and some hitherto unpublished jottings and stories by Anne Frank. Taken together, they do not make a biography, for, as I have said, the child has left only a faint trail behind her. She was gracious, capricious at times, and full of ideas. She had a tender, but also a critical spirit; a special gift for feeling deeply and for fear, but also her own special kind of courage. She had intelligence, but also many blind spots; a great deal of precocity alongside extraordinary childishness; and a sound and infrangible moral sense even in the most hopeless misery. All in all, she seems to have been what the Greeks would have called a good and beautiful person. The trail we follow here tells us a great deal, but it fails to tell us one thing: what was the source in this child of the power her name exerts throughout the world? Was this power, perhaps, not something within her, but something outside of and above her? It would be the task of a biography to explain both the person and this mystery.

We who today feel this power invoke more than the shadow of her personality when we pronounce the name of Anne Frank. We also conjure up the legend. My witnesses had a good deal to say about Anne as a person; they took account of the legend only with great reticence, or by tacitly ignoring it. Although they did not take issue with it by so much as a word, I had the impression that they were checking themselves. All of them had read Anne's diary; they did not mention it. Some had also had the courage to see the play based on the diary, but they remained taciturn whenever it was referred to. It was as though they were alienated, not by the play itself, but by the strange unsettled quality of a story that belonged to their own story. They had not entirely deciphered it yet in themselves, so that in these conversations I sometimes felt as if I were interrogating the birds to whom Francis of Assisi spoke, and they answered me: He spoke to us. What more is there to say?

For that reason Anne Frank appears here as a frailer and less dominant figure than the Anne Frank of the diary, or the Anne Frank who crosses the stage night after night somewhere in the world, entangled in life, inhabiting the ramshackle sets which represent her hiding-place, wearing a different face in every theatre, but everywhere having the same irresistible power to move us. Here I must speak of a child who was like countless other children. That must be so, for in truth she was so. Anne was a child, and not one of the witnesses claimed that she had been a prodigy, in any way out of the ordinary, moderate course of nature. She kept a diary. And she wished to live after her death.

In her diary Anne reported on approximately one-seventh of her span of life. She addressed her imaginary 'Kitty'. The seven persons who were hidden with her in the 'Secret Annexe' knew that she wrote; their clandestine visitors were also aware of it. They also knew approximately what she wrote, for sometimes Anne read aloud to them a scene from her diary, or an occasional story. Here and there in the darkness are flashes of light; but what was the whole like?

Anne wrote to Kitty:

Just imagine how interesting it would be if I were to publish a romance of the 'Secret Annexe'. The title alone would be enough to make people think it was a detective story. But, seriously, it would seem quite funny ten years after the war if we Jews were to tell how we lived and what we ate and talked about here.

The ten years are long since past. Was Anne right? Is what she has told us so unbelievable? That child, and six of the seven persons who were in hiding with her, and another five million in addition were killed.

From this entry of March 29th, 1944, then, we know that Anne toyed with the idea of publishing her diary after the war. A broadcast by a representative of the Dutch Government-in-exile, which Anne had heard the night before on the Dutch News from London, suggested the notion to her, or confirmed a secret dream she had already cherished. Among Anne's papers was found a list of fictitious names which she planned to use for the persons mentioned in the diary in case it were ever published. These fictitious names were employed in the version of the diary that was given to the world, and in order to avoid needless confusion I shall retain them in this book. But I shall also use false names or initials for my other witnesses, whom Anne did not know or did not mention. There are personal rights and private feelings which must be regarded. However, in order to ensure the authenticity of the statements recorded here, the full names and addresses of all my witnesses have been deposited with the legal representatives of the publishers Fischer Bücherei in Frankfurt.

Forty-two witnesses speak here. The fates of some will be related here, even though there are parts of their lives that seem to have nothing directly to do with Anne Frank. Nevertheless, these stories are not told for their own sake. I keep to Anne's trail. But in many places this trail is so fragile and fugitive that it would fall apart and vanish if removed from the bit of ground that it has crossed.

There is a second reason for my telling about these others.

Fate led them to Anne from the most diverse directions. Their ways all came to a focus at a single point. Thereafter all radiated away, each toward its own destination. The focal point is the meeting with Anne Frank. These radii compose the world Anne saw when she looked around.

Forty-two of seventy-six witnesses, then. En route I was given the names of a seventy-seventh and a seventy-eighth. Probably they could have been located. But there was every reason to expect them to be unrewarding witnesses, and I did not seek them out. One of the two men was possibly the betrayer of Anne Frank; the other was indisputably one of the executioners. But Anne was only one of many victims, and the betrayer and executioner only two of many betrayers and many executioners. Some of these made their confessions in the courts. All of them gave the same testimony. What could these two have added? The gap in my account cannot be closed. Or, rather, in remaining open it is closed.

CHAPTER 2

The Beginning of the Trail
and the Shadow

Before I set out on the trail of Anne Frank, I spoke to her father. He is a tall, spare man, highly intelligent, cultured, and well-educated, extremely modest and extremely kind. He survived the persecutions, but it is painful and difficult for him to talk on the subject, for he lost more than can be gained by mere survival.

The Franks were an old German-Jewish family. Otto Frank's father, a businessman, came from Landau in the Palatinate. His mother's family can be traced in the archives of Frankfurt back to the seventeenth century.

Otto Frank was born and grew up in Frankfurt am Main. He attended the Lessing Classical Secondary School, graduating with the *Abitur* (leaving-school certificate), and like his father, went into business. After the outbreak of World War I, he was assigned to an artillery company attached to the infantry. His unit consisted chiefly of surveyors and mathematicians, who as range-finders were stationed on the Western Front, in the vicinity of Cambrai, scene of many bloody, see-saw battles. Otto Frank participated in the great tank battle of Cambrai in November, 1917. His group was the first range-finding unit of the German Army to deal with the new British tanks.

The chief of the special unit to which Otto Frank was attached was named B. He is still living in Schwenningen. Frank speaks of this officer as a decent and enlightened man who handled his unit with the utmost fairness. In 1917 he proposed Frank as an officer candidate. With no background of either military training-school or special officer's course, in 1918 Otto Frank was promoted in the field to the rank of lieutenant and transferred to the hard-pressed St Quentin sector of the Front.

After the war he settled down in Frankfurt as an independent businessman, specializing in banking and the promotion of proprietary goods. He married Edith Hollander of Aachen, who died in Auschwitz in 1945. In a photograph I saw her expressive profile. She had little resemblance to Anne.

In talking with me, Otto Frank did not say one word about his relationship to Germany or to Germans. I do not think he was silent in order to spare himself, or me. Rather, it was that no explanations were called for. He was born a Jew and a German, and as long as it was honourable to do so and possible for him to be a German, he served Germany. However, he was never a nationalist. Nationalism ran counter to the Frankfurt spirit. He had had God and fatherland; he was left with only God.

He said:

"I cannot recall ever having encountered an anti-Semite in my youth in Frankfurt. Certainly there were some, but I did not meet any of them. Nor did I meet any in the Army. Of course my superior was a democratic man who would have no officers' mess or officers' orderlies in his unit. Later on, when I was a lieutenant, I tried to treat my men in the same liberal way. I can recall only one occasion in my life when I saw a German snap to attention before me. Of course that did not happen until 1944."

And an hour later this German delivered him to the Gestapo.

After his release from the Auschwitz concentration camp, Otto Frank attempted to reassemble the pieces of his old world. That proved impossible. Some few persons were living, but too many were missing. He did not give up the effort. Thus, he inserted an advertisement in a Frankfurt newspaper inquiring the whereabouts of Mrs Kati St, who had formerly been employed in his household in Frankfurt.

I visited Frau Kati in Höchst in June 1957. While she was explaining how her sister had seen the newspaper notice and had let her know of it, her husband looked among various papers on the bookshelf and produced a red folder labelled 'Anne Frank'. He laid it before me on the table. Kati and her husband had collected everything that bore on the Franks – newspaper clippings, reviews of the Frankfurt performances of *The Diary of Anne Frank*, theatre tickets, an invitation to the celebration of Anne's birthday on June 12th, 1957, in St Paul's Church, an excerpt from Eugen Kogon's speech on that occasion. But their collection dated from a time long before public memorials for Anne and stage performances; they had been gathering mementos since before the war. There were photographs and letters from Aachen and Amsterdam in the folder; there was also the note from Otto Frank written in February 1952 when they responded to his advertisement: 'I am so wrought up, thinking of you, that I can say very little now. I will tell you the whole story when we see each other. Neither my wife nor the children are alive; all fell victim to the Nazis. I alone remain.'

Kati smiles and weeps all at once; there is no gulf between the smile which is meant for the stranger and the tears she weeps as she thinks of those who are gone. Kati is a pretty woman, probably around fifty. She beams whether she is smiling or weeping. Until her marriage in 1929 she was the mainstay of the Franks' household. Even after marriage she frequently came to help out in case of illness or other emergencies. She was in the house at Margot's birth, and watched Margot grow up; she was likewise in the house when

Anne came into the world. But she remembers Margot more distinctly, and showed me pictures of the elder sister. Margot had always been the beauty of the two, as well as the gentle and well-behaved child. Out of the photograph a fair, regular-featured, almost angelic face gazed at me.

Kati could not say very much about Anne, whom she had known only as a small child. There was, she said, great commotion in the house when Anne was born. Mrs Frank went to hospital, and had a difficult delivery. But on June 12th, in the morning, Mr Frank telephoned Kati at last to say that it was another girl, and that all had gone well.

I told Kati that in the hospital records 'the birth of a male child' was recorded. Kati laughed at that. That showed how tired the nurse must have been after the long night, she exclaimed. Anne had not arrived until half past seven in the morning. But a boy, a boy? Kati smiled and shook her head. Oh no...

But then it occurred to her that after all there was something of the boy about Anne. Margot was always the little princess. She was neat and careful; except for her underclothes, she might have gone on wearing the same clothes for a week. It was as though dirt did not exist for her, Kati said. There was something almost unnatural about it, but dirt simply did not touch her; and Kati said, she always feared for this child, although she did not know why.

But Anne was the exact opposite of Margot. She had to be completely changed every day, sometimes twice a day. For example, one morning Kati found her sitting on the balcony in the rain, in the middle of a puddle, chortling with delight. A good scolding left the little girl unaffected. She did not even offer to get up out of the puddle. She wanted Kati to tell her a story right there and then, and it made no difference that Kati had no time. The story could be a short one, she said.

Kati lost patience. She picked Anne up, carried her into the nursery and set her firmly down on the table to change her clothes.

But then Kati remembers something else. She breaks her story to say:

"Above the nursery table hung a handsome lamp. It was very big, and Mr Frank had had it painted with animals. A regular zoo it was, and Anne would always look up at it. She had all sorts of stories about the animals."

Kati returns to the photographs. She shows me one of Anne in a little white coat in front of a public building. ("God knows how long the coat stayed white that day" – Kati shakes her head.) Then Anne as a baby – and another of Anne as a baby, sitting on her grandmother's lap. Mrs Frank is standing near by, and Kati, too, is visible in the photograph; she had not changed much over the years. Margot is cuddling against her knee. Anne is pouting and looking up mistrustfully. But who is the third child in the picture?

"That is Gertrud," Kati says. "Imagine, I had not seen her for almost twenty-five years. But last week in St Paul's Church…"

That afternoon I visited Gertrud, who is now Mrs Gertrud T. She confirmed the fact that, until their recent encounter, it was nearly twenty-five years since she had last seen Kati.

That quarter of a century has made Gertrud into a grown woman who has children of her own as old as Margot and Anne were then. The twenty-five years have erased some memories, but left others so bright that it sometimes seems, Gertrud says, that it all happened yesterday. She recalls well the last time she saw the Franks. They were leaving Germany after the issuing of the decree that Jewish children could no longer attend the same schools as non-Jewish children – for that was how it began. And Gertrud recalls that Mr Frank spoke little at the time. He had always done silently whatever had to be done, as long as she had known him, although in other respects he was not a withdrawn man; rather of a merry and jocular temperament. And to think that such people as the Franks had to be the victims, Gertrud says, people who were the soul of kindness.

It struck me that Gertrud used much the same language as Kati. In spite of the ten years' difference in age, the two women resemble one another, at least in their warmth and friendliness. Perhaps they are not objective witnesses, for they loved the Franks. But love always makes a selection among its objects and to that extent it is objective.

Selection – it has become an ugly word. The Franks, too, were 'selected' – for that was what it was called when the mother was separated from her children. After this 'selection' both mother and children died, hundreds of miles apart.

Gertrud's family lived on Marbachweg, near the Franks. A playmate of the children, Gertrud used to see them every day, and continued to visit frequently after 1930, when the Franks moved to Ganghoferstrasse. The Franks also called on Gertrud's parents, and one day, when the families were sitting over coffee, Anne regarded Gertrud's father fixedly, with a frowning expression, and suddenly exclaimed across the table:

"Why, you have eyes like a cat."

Gertrud's father had laughed heartily, but the others were somewhat embarrassed. For there was a good deal of truth in Anne's observation – only, of course, that was not the sort of thing to say.

At this point a curious tale must be told. Kati unfolded it to me, and Gertrud corroborated it. It seems that there were more than four members in the Frank family. There were two additional invisible occupants of the household with whom everyone was familiar. No one could remember who had first discovered them in the nursery; Mr Frank fancied that perhaps it was he himself, but he could not be sure. At any rate, there was no doubt about their existence; even the grandmothers and friends of the family were on intimate terms with them.

These remarkable beings were already in the house at the time of Anne's birth, so that she made their acquaintance early and learned to reckon with them – for they could not be ignored. They were two household sprites of variable age but invariable characters. Both were named Paula. They were distinguished as Good Paula and Bad Paula. Although invisible, they grew up along with Margot, and after Anne's birth they began at the beginning again and grew up with her. The only way to tell them apart was by their acts. For example, Good Paula always polished her plate, while Bad Paula would fiddle with her spoon and make faces when she did not like something. It would occur only to Bad Paula to pull the legs from a fly. That was just the sort of thing she would do. Good Paula, on the other hand, was sweet and well-behaved, and would never so much as pull her sister's hair, as other little girls sometimes did.

In other words, the Franks had their private Shock-headed Peter, and both Paulas proved useful companions, although not much could be learned from them of the interplay between acts and rewards. They were as they were, the good one good and the bad one bad; they displayed good and evil as it occurs in the world. They had no one to praise or reprimand them for their acts. In this respect their moral role differed from that of Shock-headed Peter. Neither of the Paulas was an example; they denoted possibilities, between which a child could choose. Margot knew from the start which Paula she should be like, but Anne had some difficulty along these lines. She was attached to both these strange friends, to both at once. Of course Anne, too, knew which Paula she preferred, but sometimes she was intrigued by the other one, and so both Paulas remained faithfully at her side for a long time. She went her way between them; it was somewhat of a zigzag course as she veered now toward the one, now toward the other. And gradually, without her noticing, the two Paulas became the two Annes, Anne and her other self, what she called 'the ordinary Anne' and the 'second Anne'. 'Kitty' was to learn later, from so many diary communications, how hard it is to be singlehearted when one has dealings with two Paulas.

Anne never entirely forgot her erstwhile companions. Among the papers found with the diary was one dated December 22nd, 1943:

When I was small, Pim always used to tell me about Bad Paula. There were many different stories, and I could not hear enough of them. Now, when I am with him at night…

… Those were the fearsome nights of the next to last winter of the war, when fleets of planes came over Amsterdam and the old house on the Prinsengracht shook from the reverberations of the anti-aircraft guns…

… he sometimes tells me about Paula again, and I have written down his latest story…

A page-long story follows. But there is no longer any mention of a Good and a Bad Paula; only one is left, a girl as old as Anne now is. Good and Bad have merged into a small living person who is no longer invisible. It is wartime in this story – a different war, to be sure, but Paula, too, is in distress and must flee, for she has fallen into the hands of the Russians. Some elements of this story are so fantastic that they might well be true; others so plausible that we feel them to be invented. It is a story of World War I that Otto Frank told Anne, and may well contain as much realism as most improvised tales. In the end, at any rate, everything turns out well. Paula succeeds in escaping and returns home to her parents in Frankfurt. But before that there is a moment when Paula, abandoned in Russia, sighs:

What queer people these Russians are! Now they are leaving me here to my fate in a foreign country. I know the Germans would act differently in such a situation...

And Anne added in parentheses:

After all, we must remember that Paula was a German girl...

Kati said to me:

"It must have been 1929, we were doing a big wash. The washerwoman came early in the morning, and was in a temper, and when I asked her, 'What's the matter, Mrs Zollinger?' she said, 'I didn't get a wink of sleep all night. There was a big racket in the street again.' 'What was up?' I asked. And she said: 'The Brownshirts were fighting and making a row again.'

"Later, at lunch, I asked Mr Frank who these Brownshirts were. And, you know, Mr Frank just laughed and tried to make a joke of the whole thing, and although it wasn't very much of a laugh and not much of a joke, he did try. But Mrs Frank looked up from her plate, she did, and she fixed her eyes on us and said: 'We'll find out soon enough who they are, Kati.' And that was no joke, and it wasn't said like a joke."

Gertrud recollected:

"Mr Frank never spoke about anything that troubled him. But sometimes you could see the way it was worrying him and working inside him."

Otto Frank told me:

"On January 30th [1933] we happened to be visiting friends. We were sitting at the table and listening to the radio. First came the news that Hitler had become Chancellor. Then came an account of the storm troopers' torch parade in Berlin, and we heard the shouting and cheers, and the announcer said that Hindenburg was standing at the window, waving. At the end Hitler made his 'Give me four years' speech. Our host said cheerfully: 'Well, let's see what the man can do!'

"I could not reply, and my wife sat as if she were turned to stone."

Kati's husband planted himself in front of me, and spoke up with suppressed passion. "In one respect Anne was wrong in her diary," he said. "People are not good and it is not possible to believe in them."

The Franks left Frankfurt in the summer of 1933. Otto Frank went directly to Holland to seek a new means of livelihood, while Mrs Frank temporarily moved in with her mother in Aachen, keeping the children with her.

Gertrud and Kati have saved many letters of those years, all of them in Edith Frank's large, old-fashioned, ornate hand. There is a card to Kati written shortly after arrival in Aachen. It must have been handled by Anne before being sent, for a big pencilled scribble covers the entire face of it.

A subsequent letter to Gertrud reads:

'Anne reminds me of you in her fondness for babies. She peeks into every pram we pass. If she had her way, she would take every toddler she sees for a walk.'

From Holland, in March 1934:

'Since December we have had a small flat in Amsterdam. We had Margot with us at Christmas, and Anne has just come. They stayed in Aachen for exactly a year. Both children are full of fun. Anne a little comedian.'

There are birthday and New Year greetings, little notes of reply or thanks. There is little information, as if exchange of news were not necessary among friends who think of one another with so much affection. Sometimes, however, a word is dropped that sounds quite another key.

'Margot is happy in school and Anne loves her kindergarten...' 'We too are well. The children have recuperated splendidly here and Anne in particular has become very strong.'

After Anne's birthday in June 1935:

'The child had a gorgeous party, first in kindergarten, which she loves going to now, and then with the children at home.' Many dear, kind letters came from Frankfurt, Aachen and Basel.

'During the school holidays I was at the seashore with the children... Anne is learning to swim with great pleasure. Her health is much better this year.'

'Anne is going to the Montessori School. She is not so well-behaved as Margot, and does not like to buckle down to things.' 'Do you know that Margot's and Anne's favourite game is your quincto?' (Gertrud, who sent the game to them, recalls dimly that it was some kind of card game.)

'Anne is struggling with her reading lessons. Margot has a great deal of schoolwork...'

(Under this note is Anne's first literary effort: 'hello anne,' pencilled in neat little letters.) 'The children adore the wrappers and proudly wear them every day.'

'Our big girl is very hard-working and already thinks of

going on to college; little Anne is somewhat less industrious, but very droll… witty and amusing…' (I asked Gertrud whether she could still recall the wrappers she had made for the children at the time. She pondered, then shook her head. I told her that there is still preserved in Amsterdam a small wrapper which had belonged to Anne, made of beige, flower printed silk with red trimming and ribbons. Gertrud looked wide-eyed at me. She said, "Why, that can't be…or do you think it's really possible?")

On July 14th, 1937, Edith Frank wrote to Kati St, whose husband had been arrested and sent to prison for membership in a 'seditious workers' group:

'We think often of you and your grief…'

From 1938 on the letters were rarer and briefer. It was necessary to be careful, for foreign mail was being censored. After the summer of 1939 there were no more letters. The war had broken out.

After my visit to Gertrud I went on to the houses on Marbachweg and Ganghoferstrasse. The house in which Anne spent the first year of her life, 307 Marbachweg, is a yellow, two-storey, stucco-covered building with pale green shutters and a tall birch in the front garden.

Little has changed in this street since 1929, I felt. Possibly bombs may have fallen here, for Frankfurt was much bombed, but I found no traces of the recent past except for an air-raid shelter still standing on the corner of Kaiser Sigmund Strasse. It has been capped with a superfluous tile roof and has had false windows painted in white upon rainbow-coloured walls. Perhaps the citizens hoped thus to assimilate the building into its surroundings. But the well-meaning subterfuge is a failure. Time was when an air-raid shelter stood in the street; now there is a gaudy phantom.

A memorial plaque to Anne has recently been affixed to

the other house, 24 Ganghoferstrasse. Since neighbours were looking out of the windows, I made a pretence of copying the text of the plaque into my notebook, thus accounting for the fact that I was stationed for some time before the house. After I had been standing there for a few minutes, an elderly gentleman came up to me, took up a position half behind my elbow, and compared what I was writing to the text on the plaque. I clapped my notebook shut, and we looked at one another.

"Do you live here?" I asked him.

"No, but near by."

"You've lived here long?" I asked.

"Yes." He tilted his head a little to one side. "But I did not know her. There are too many children in this neighbourhood. See."

He pointed to the opposite pavement, where a band of children engaged in some game were trotting by.

"I have been thinking about it ever since I first heard," he said. "But there were always so many children."

CHAPTER 3

When We Were Still in Normal Life

In the spring of 1957 a curious incident took place in Jerusalem. The young wife of a Government employee – an average housewife with several small children and a limited budget, whose days were chiefly spent in the kitchen between the stove, the refrigerator, and the washing machine, who went out possibly once a month to the movies – one woman like thousands of others, that is, found herself besieged by radio and newspaper reporters. She was eagerly questioned, asked to pose with the President, for photographs, while hordes of people pressed around her in hopes of getting a glimpse of her face. All this excitement took place in the Habimah theatre shortly after a youthful actress, during the performance, had fixed her eyes upon the darkness beyond the footlights and exclaimed:

"Yesterday evening, before I fell asleep, who should suddenly appear before my eyes but Lies! I saw her in front of me, clothed in rags, her face thin and worn. Her eyes were very big and she looked so sadly and reproachfully at me that I could read in her eyes: 'Oh, Anne, why have you deserted me?'... Lies, is she still alive? What is she doing? Oh, God, protect her and bring her back to us. Lies, I see in you all the time what my lot might have been, I keep seeing myself in your place..."

These lines from Anne Frank's diary had been inserted into the play for that one evening – and Lies, who was sitting beside her husband in the tenth row of the stalls, gripped his hand and watched the tragedy on the stage, shaken and breathless. But oddly enough, she said later, she had felt no special closeness to the actress on the stage. She had tried to explain this to the reporters:

"After all, I knew the Franks. But these people were actors, and I could not forget for a moment that I was sitting in a theatre. Anne and I were very close friends, you must understand that, and yet no one suspected that she could write. With Margot it would have been different. We thought Margot terribly talented and capable of anything. But Anne, you see, was just my friend, and we sat side by side in the Montessori school in Amsterdam for six years, and whispered in class, and the teacher could never separate us, no matter how hard she tried. And later, when we went to the Jewish Lyceum, I was called out the very first day, and put in another class. I felt utterly miserable; I didn't know a soul in this class. But next morning, the door opened and Anne slipped on to the bench beside me. Nobody said anything to her, and so we stayed together until she suddenly disappeared..."

This story is not intended to cast doubt on the stage version of the *Diary*. Reality and the art that has arisen out of it do not run counter to each other, for they are connected by threads at once far stronger and far more delicate than mere logic, historical correctness and identities. I relate it only because it shows how honest Anne's friends and witnesses are, how little they have been seduced by the prospect of sharing in the fame of her legend. Lies P could say, to the disappointment of reporters: "But Anne, you see, was just my friend." She remained loyal to her memories and to the simplicities of childhood, and she was truthful enough to say that she had seen no omens of greatness or of a great destiny. Anne and Lies were free and happy in Amsterdam. It would have been embroidering the truth to describe that period as a drama fraught with foreshadowings. Anne and her friends enjoyed themselves – that is all. Happiness is not the stuff of which novels are made.

In one of the notebooks which she kept along with her diary, Anne wrote:

When we were still in normal life, everything was tremendous...

I have translated this sentence quite literally. We must understand that the word 'tremendous' is school jargon; it was a fashionable expression among the children of Amsterdam-Zuid, like 'super' elsewhere. It meant that something was wonderful and fine and splendid; the children shied away from the usual high-flown words, choosing instead words so high-flown that no one could possibly take them literally. The passage continues:

I could tell about school for hours, about our pranks, about the boys in class...

She then does go on telling about these things for a few pages, but by no means 'for hours' – and given Anne's fluency, a few pages mean little. She addresses Kitty, her secret confidante:

Do you remember how one day I came home from town, and there was a package in the letterbox for me "d'un ami R"? It could not be from anyone but Rob, and inside the package was a brooch, a real stylish one, from his father's store. I wore it for three days; then it broke.

And do you remember how Lies and I peached on the class... and then had to write a long begging letter so that they'd make up with us again?

Do you remember how Pim P said to Rob in the tram, so loud that Sanne heard it and passed it on to me: Anne is lots prettier than Danka L, especially when she laughs. And how Rob answered him back: You're too nosy for your own good!

And do you remember how Maurice wanted to call on my father and ask him whether he could go out with his daughter?...

And how Rob and Anne Frank always wrote letters to each other when Rob was in the hospital?

And how Sam rode behind me on the bicycle and offered me his arm?...

And how Bram gave me a kiss on the cheek when I promised that I'd never tell anybody about him and Trees L?

After this last question mark Anne suddenly felt prompted to go on in block letters, and wrote:

HOW I WISH THAT THESE CAREFREE
SCHOOLDAYS WOULD COME AGAIN.

As I read these pages I felt that Anne, in the dreary confinement and enforced silence of her hiding-place in the Secret Annexe, had completely combed through her memories of those happy years, looking for stories by which she would be able to summon back those years and so possess them, only to discover that in happy times, there are no such stories. Certainly there were none that could cast even a glimmer of light upon such a strange adventure as the one Anne was now experiencing and which she alone seemed to see as an adventure – she alone of the eight people locked up with her. And I believe that Lies P. in Jerusalem was also considering the frailty of memories when she drew a sharp distinction between the happy times and the tragedy, and when she sought to protect the former from the latter – she who herself had gone through a concentration-camp experience scarcely less horrible than Anne's and who, as she said, had been "just" Anne's friend.

*

Normal life, then, and *just friends* and *these carefree schooldays* – such was Anne's existence from 1934 to 1942. These happy times actually continued until 1942, although the German invasion of the Netherlands had come on May 10th, 1940, and although the avalanche of anti-Jewish laws started fifty-three days later. But Anne and Lies had careful parents, and the people of Amsterdam did everything they could to shield the many Jewish children in their midst as long as possible. Those children knew very well the menace that hung over them, and what was going on all around them; but for the time being they were protected and among friends.

Lies's father, who had been Press chief of the last pre-Nazi administration in Prussia, had emigrated to Holland with his family in 1933. They now lived near the Franks on Merwedeplein in Amsterdam-Zuid, one of the big, modern, bright suburbs which the city had thrust out toward the marshes. These were neighbourhoods of broad streets, lined with simple, attractive terrace houses with those great big Dutch windows which always give the impression that they were meant not so much for looking out as for looking in.

Merwedeplein is a large square with an immense children's playground in the centre. I retraced the walk Anne, in her diary for June 30th, 1942, speaks of having taken. It leads along the south side of Merwedeplein, then through a narrow alley and along the edge of Victoriaplein to Rooseveltlaan, as the splendid boulevard is now named. Finally I went by way of Waalstraat back to Merwedeplein. The whole walk takes eleven minutes – allowing time for a glance into Titus Kasper's watch shop and into the bookstore on the corner of Waalstraat. Anne's walk to the Montessori school on Niersstraat required no longer. Nor did I forget to stop for strawberry ice cream at the Oasis – '*we usually finish up with a visit to the nearest ice-cream shop...*

where Jews are allowed', as Anne wrote in 1942. But the shop has changed owners, and the new owner knows nothing about the former clientele.

Anne used to roam this neighbourhood with her girl friends, with Rob (who had given her the brooch), with Harry Goldberg, her last friend in 'normal life'. And on the corner *'there stood Peter Wessel with two other boys'*; he greeted her and it was *'the first time'* he had spoken to her *'for ages';* Anne was *'really pleased'.* Everywhere in this neighbourhood she was shielded by the clean, bright, uniform respectability of the quarter. Scenes of tragedies do not look thus, and it is strange now to go through these streets knowing what happened there. Margot, Anne, Sanne, Peter Wessel – they are all dead. But pavements have no conscience; they show no trace. The boys still swoop by on their bicycles; the teenage girls dismount and stand gossiping when they meet one another; from the handlebars their schoolbags swing; on every corner the charming, trivial, everyday chatter can be heard, plans for tomorrow and tomorrow afternoon, and "Have you done the third example yet? What's your answer?" And it is June now, just as it was when Anne took that stroll with Harry; and not until I made this tour a second time did I discover in the bookshop on the corner of Waalstraat – where fifteen years ago Mr Frank bought the red-checked diary for Anne's birthday – her picture in the window. Three copies of her book stand side by side on display – and that is the only testimony that she ever lived. In the Secret Annexe Anne wrote a story whose scene is laid in these pleasant, bright streets.

Riek

At fifteen after four I walked down to a fairly quiet street, and had just decided to go to the nearest pastry shop when two girls came out

46

of a side street, chattering animatedly, and continuing on in the same direction as myself.

It is amusing and interesting to everyone to listen to the conversation of two teenagers, not only because they laugh at the slightest trifles, but because their laughter is so infectious that you can't help laughing with them. I am affected just that way. As I walked along behind the two friends, I heard them discussing what sweets they ought to buy for their ten cents...By the time they reached the shop, they had not come to any agreement, but I could guess, as soon as I glanced into the window, which pastries they were going to choose. It was not very crowded inside the store. They were served right away, and came out again with two big cakes which they had not yet bitten into – that was a sheer miracle.

Half a minute later I also had bought my pastry, and saw the two still walking ahead of me, still deep in talk.

At the next corner there was another bakery, and in front of the window stood a little girl staring with longing eyes at the confections on display. The two lucky owners of the cakes stopped beside her to look into the window, and quickly fell into conversation with the poor child. I came around the corner just in time to catch the last of it.

"Are you so very hungry?" one of the girls asked the child. "Would you like a piece of cake too?"

The little girl nodded.

But then the other girl exclaimed: "Don't be silly, Riek. Just eat your cake up as I'm doing. If you let her bite into it, it will spoil the taste for you."

Riek did not answer. She glanced from her cake to the child, and could not make up her mind, but then she gave the child a pat and the cake, and said kindly,

"Here take the whole thing. I have to go home for supper anyway."

And before the child could even thank her, the two girls were gone around the corner. The child was taking large bites out of her cake when I passed, and said:

"Would you like a taste, Miss? Somebody gave it to me…"

I tried to locate Anne's old friends, and did find three of them.

Trees L only laughed when she heard the story about Bram, and that Anne had promised not to tell. She could not remember what it was all about. But then, Trees was older than Anne, was in fact a member of Margot's class. Naturally she had little idea of the gossip that circulated among the younger girls.

Toosje K is now a young woman. From Toosje I learned that they used to play *hinkelen* outside the door at Merwedeplein. Hinkelen sounds like a kind of hopscotch, with squares marked in chalk on the pavement, the problem being to hop into certain squares, while shunning others. I was prepared for something of the sort, for I had seen a photograph showing Lies and Anne on the pavement, Anne crouching and drawing the chalk lines. On the other hand, I learned for the first time that the children of the neighbourhood were keen on turning cartwheels and that handstands were the rage for a long while. Though these, Toosje confesses, were done against the wall of some building, the important thing was how long you could stand on your hands, rather than any special grace of execution. Unfortunately, Anne was grievously unskilful at such games, Toosje reported. She always sagged at once, lost her balance, and tumbled over. Of course she was certainly a good deal smaller than Toosje, and several months younger as well, but one day she said to her friend with admirable objectivity:

"That's still no reason not to be able to do a handstand."

It occurred to Toosje to mention that Anne had had

another grief: she could not whistle. She simply could not learn, no matter how determinedly she practised on the stairs and out on Merwedeplein. And you *had* to be able to whistle, Toosje explained, because as children they had never rung the house bell when they wanted to call on one another. They whistled; that was settled. And now there was Anne, left out… "And do you know what she did?" Toosje asked. "She sang instead."

Toosje sang Anne's call to me, overcoming an embarrassment that made her flush red to the tips of her ears, and blink, and look off at a secret point that was not at all inside the room. "Lalalalala," she sang, and again, "Lalalalala" – five notes, five thirds, up and down. The second time she even placed her hands over her mouth so that it would sound as it had sounded then, when Anne would sing through the letterbox slit. That was how it had sounded, exactly like that. Toosje's mother nodded agreement.

When after a while the conversation began to lag, I thought to ask Toosje whether she had seen the play. She shook her head briefly, and her mother said: "No, Toosje and I didn't go. You know we had Anne's tomcat, Moortje, with us all through the war. So we just didn't want to go. My elder daughter was the only one of us who accepted the invitation. But she did not give us any report on it."

It was late evening before I found my way out to Amsterdam-West, where Jopie van der Waal now lives.

Lies was Anne's best friend, and Jopie was Anne's best friend. There is no contradiction here, for best friends are so rare that anyone should be glad to have two of them – nor should we forget Sanne Houtmann, who was also Anne's best friend. After all, there are fluctuations in the barometer of friendship. A compass, too, does not always point due north. Therefore it is good to be well provided. Moreover, Anne later confessed in one of her random notes: *'But I have never had a real friend'.*

That place was reserved for Kitty, for the true friend in need. But in 'normal life' the best friends served, and one of them proved her worth in time of misfortune as well.

I was out of luck and did not find Jopie at home. She had gone out with her husband, leaving her baby rosily asleep in its crib, while her mother sat guard over its slumber. But Madame van der Waal quickly observed that perhaps it was not such bad luck after all, since mothers have a better memory than children.

Madame van der Waal, French by birth, married a Dutchman and has been living in Amsterdam since she was quite young. But to this day she cannot really manage Dutch. It gratified her to hear that I could not really manage it either, and she simply ignored my objection that my French was scarcely better.

"Anne?" she said. "Aaah, Anne was a little monkey. *Très intelligent, très féminine...* And just thirteen, consider that!" Madame exclaimed, clapping her hands over her breast. "She was a great personality. A human soul. *Une femme!* Why, recently I went to Bijenkorf – that is the big department store on the Damrak – and all of a sudden I saw Anne's picture right in front of me. Not in the book department, not a bit of it. It stood on an ordinary shelf, with a few flowers alongside it, and in front of it the sales-girl sold me thread... No, I tell you," Madame said, shaking her finger as if she were protesting against the invisible Dark Angel in the air, "we have not lost her."

There was no need for me to put questions to Madame.

What she had to say came tumbling out of her.

Jopie had seen the play, on opening night. She had sat near the Queen and she had reported that the Queen's face had been deeply flushed from excitement and emotion. "And now, I ask you, Anne was only a child, after all. Remember that, a child!

"I myself," Madame continued, "have only read her diary, but when I read it Anne appeared before me. I saw her, alive. But she had not come to me, no, it was not like that. She drew me to her, to herself, into her strange, grotesque world which none of us knew a thing about. No – suddenly Madame's voice became strong and positive – "she is not lost to us. Jopie admits I'm right. There's Jopie's baby sleeping over there. Have you seen it? To think that here we already have the next generation."

Madame delighted me. She was in her sixties, with grey hair which at the moment was somewhat disarrayed; her eyes flashed as she talked with me. Her embroidery lay untouched in her lap. There was something sweet, knowing, artful, and grandmotherly about her mouth as she chattered freely away. And she was not repeating a tale she had told over a dozen times. No journalists had called on her as yet. She spoke straight from the heart, expressing herself by gestures now and then. I took out my notebook because I wanted to have her exact phrases, and half concealed it behind the table as I wrote. But this caution was unnecessary. Madame paid no attention to what I was doing. She raised her finger, and went on:

"Do you know when I saw Anne for the last time? In my own flat. I had made a blue knitted dress for her. When it was ready, she came for it. Naturally we tried it on once more – it looked sweet on her, and I told her so. And what do you think Anne said to that? 'Why of course,' she said; 'after all, it's brand new.'"

Madame van der Waal is a dressmaker by trade, and even at night she does not entirely put aside her dressmaking. I am not referring to her quick, darting hands, nor to the embroidery in her lap; but she moves her head as if she were continually taking measurements of her own words; she studies the style and the fit with blinking eyes; and sometimes her fingers flash to her mouth as though she had a few pins pursed between her lips, so that if necessary she can take a tuck here or there.

She told me that Anne had been a gifted customer – believe it or not, there are such things, she said. There are gifted customers just as there are some very stupid ones. But Anne, she knew very well when something did not fit, and she would say it right out, and no bit of pulling in back or in front would satisfy her. "Aaah!" Madame exclaimed, "she knew who she was. That's it."

I looked startled for a moment, since Madame van der Waal was the first person to say anything like that to me. She sensed at once that this was something arresting.

"Don't you believe it?"

She eyed me sharply.

I quickly asked whether she could remember what colour Anne's eyes were. Her father had told me that they were light, I said, but he had been unable to describe them more closely. Madame answered tersely and explicitly: "She had grey-green eyes. Like a cat…" she added as the same word shot into my mind, but she instantly gave it a twist as she continued: "Only cats have veiled eyes, and Anne's were very candid. That is the difference. She could see things – and how! She saw everything exactly as it was, and sometimes she would make a remark – sharp as a needle. Only it did not hurt, because she always hit exactly to the point.

"Margot was entirely different. You would never imagine that two persons could be so very different. Margot was always – *summa cum laude*, all through school, all through life. She, too, was candid and decided, but she was quiet and kind. She was such an exceptional girl that I was always speechless with her. But Anne took after her grandmother, and after her Great-aunt Frank. She was capricious – oh, how capricious!

"You ask whether I had any idea what a writer Anne was? Why, of course. She always wanted to be a writer. No, I wasn't surprised for a moment when I heard about her diary, nor when I saw it. Anne was a personality, you understand. And what a personality! Why should such a personality not be able to write, too?"

Madame beamed, and I granted the point, since this is a very broad subject. Whereupon Madame continued:

"She might have gone into the movies, too, of course. Why not? She not only had a gift for being somebody; she also had a gift for impersonation. My husband was electrified every time she came in at the door – and yet he had two daughters of his own. But the difference was that Anne knew who she was. Our girls didn't. Not even Jopie. Have you seen Jopie?"

Madame rose from the sofa and fetched two pictures from the chest of drawers. There was Jopie during her schooldays – a sweet child with wondering eyes. And Jopie as a bride – a brunette beauty with a tiny face, a wedding veil covering her hair and fluttering over her shoulders as it was blown by the hymeneal wind of Amsterdam.

Madame took the photographs back from me, and as she held them to the light and looked at them again, she said:

"But Jopie never did know who she was, and yet the two of them were such good friends. They were like a pair of lovers. But Anne had *charme* and self-assurance, while Jopie was *froide, timide*... And still, the plotting and whispering that was always going on between the two of them, and the telephoning all day long, though the Franks lived not three doors away from us. Every morning, there was the telephone ringing – and fifteen minutes later they would be seeing each other in school anyhow. But they never could wait that long.

"When Jopie went to the theatre and saw Anne again – the girl must have been wonderful, fascinating, that other girl on the stage – Jopie couldn't say a word when she came home. She went right to bed… She never was really able to express herself, not even as a child, but nevertheless they were like a pair of lovers with one another. And if Anne spent the weekend with Lies – what jealousy! Indescribable. But if she did not go to see Lies, she came to us, or Jopie went over to the Franks. When Anne came to stay with us, she always brought a suitcase. A suitcase, mind you, when it wasn't a stone's throw between us. The suitcase was empty of course, but Anne insisted on it, because only with the suitcase did she feel as if she were really travelling. And before they went to sleep, the whispering and giggling…"

But suddenly Madame drooped a little. She seemed to be looking into herself. After a moment she said:

"You know what has just come to me? I still have the folding bed she used to sleep on. Jopie's was the one we gave away…"

A second passed. I checked my notes. Then I heard Madame's voice:

"So you think Anne did not know who she was?"

Twirling the pencil between my fingers, I replied, "Oh, that is hard to say."

Another moment passed in silence, and I looked toward the window, where night was coming on – as much as night can come in June; it was a darkness full of hidden colours. Then Madame laughed again:

"She knew. Just think, one Sunday, we were just about to sit down to the table, Anne suddenly said goodbye. I said: 'Why, Anne, we're going to eat now.' But she said no, she had to go home because she had to give Moortje his bath.

And I said: 'Why, Anne, you're crazy. A cat isn't supposed to be bathed.' But Anne said haughtily: 'Why not? I've often bathed him, and he's never said anything about it!' And she took her suitcase and left.

"Oh no," Madame concluded, "she knew what she wanted. Believe me, she did. And she knew who she was, too."

Thus said Madame van der Waal.

I had to wait a short while until the director of the kindergarten of the Montessori school on Niersstraat could see me. It is now called the Anne Frank school. The three connecting playrooms were each in charge of a young teacher, but everything was in a whirl, with children perched on hassocks, sitting at tables, squatting on mats, with coloured pencils darting across paper, towers of building blocks mounting toward heaven. In one corner a glockenspiel tinkled. Long and short letters were being read, written; long and short arithmetic examples reckoned; and amid it all the children were laughing and sometimes squabbling, but everything was being done very quietly; there was something almost strange about the quiet. The director pointed to a small five-year-old boy who had decided to write all the numbers from one to a thousand on a tiny roll of paper, one neatly under the other. At the moment this dogged systematician had reached 638. The young teacher said:

"Two years ago we had another boy like that."

But the director took the matter seriously.

"Let him write if he wants to, I say," she said to me. "By doing it, he gets it over with soonest. Why should we do anything to oppose him? That would be wrong.

"But Paty, come here please, show us your letter!"

Paty, at the next table but one, is the brown-haired child. She hung back for the briefest moment, then gave me the letter and watched me sharply as I read. She had written:

"naughty marja!

"how are you? Are you coming today? Guess what I saw on the calendar when I woke up? It's my birthday! whee!"

"Well that calls for congratulations," I said.

Paty accepted her congratulations and flounced a bit until the director interposed:

"Why no. We had your birthday two weeks ago."

At that Paty laughed slyly and took back her letter to continue it. The director said:

"It was her sixth birthday, so that now she'll be going to school. They all leave here when they reach six."

Suddenly she recalled the purpose of my visit, but she did not know what she could say:

"So many years have passed, you know, and after so many years with children all the faces merge into one child's face. Do you know what I mean? In the past it would bother me when I suddenly realized that I had forgotten a face and simply could not recall it, but now I think this is as it should be. They keep coming all the time. Every year... Now look at that; I knew it would happen..."

At this point the high, multicoloured tower of building blocks collapsed with a clatter.

School and kindergarten are in the same building; I had only to climb one flight of stairs. Mr van G, Anne's first-grade teacher, said to me:

"No, I can say only what I have said before: she was no prodigy. She was likable, healthy, perhaps a little delicate, though I believe that showed up later on. She certainly was not an extraordinary child, not even ahead of her age. Or perhaps I should put it this way: in many things she was very mature, but on the other hand, in other things she was unusually childish. The combination of these two characteristics made her very attractive. There are many potentialities in such a mixture, after all.

"My route to school in the mornings was the same as hers, and we often walked together, and went on doing so long after she had passed out of my class. Sometimes she told me stories and poems which she had made up together with her father when they went out for strolls. These were always very jolly stories. She told me a great deal about her father, and very little about her sister or her mother.

"It is correct that she wanted to be a writer. That I remember. It started early with her, very early... and I imagine she might very well have become one. She was able to *experience* more than other children, if you know what I mean. I might almost put it that she heard more, the soundless things too, and sometimes she heard things whose very existence we have almost forgotten. That happens with children, you know. And so she might have..."

The scene in the class for the eleven to thirteen-year-olds is really not much different from that down below in the kindergarten. The same gaiety, the same peculiar quiet. Of course there is no squabbling in this class, and the towers reaching to heaven are no longer of building blocks, but of ideas and poems. Reckoning is not done with beads, but with the rules of algebra, which are not quite so easy to grasp.

Anne was in this class until 1941, shortly before her twelfth birthday. Her class teacher was Mrs K, the principal of the school. She wrote in her diary:

It was at the end of the school year, I was in form 6B, when I had to say goodbye to Mrs K. We both wept, it was very sad.

Mrs K is a tall, slender, warm-hearted woman. She said:

"I was so anxious to keep Anne another year. She was still

very young for the class, and very frail also. She had been ill for a while…"

She showed me the class rolls for the years 1935–41. These are really only lists of the children present; each child receives two check marks for each day, one for the morning and one for the afternoon. There I saw the three or four thousand checks entered for Anne during those six years. But during the years 1936 and 1937 there were many blanks in the series. Mrs K explained:

"She had had measles, and afterwards she had some sort of heart trouble. That was the period when she was called 'Tenderfoot', both here in school and at home. But she recovered very nicely, and during her last years here she was in good health. But the name stuck for quite a while. You can see from this list that she and Lies were friends. Look here. We had only two cases of measles. Lies was sick from December 5th on, and Anne from the tenth. They were always together, of course.

"But I cannot recall," Mrs K said, "that the two chattered so much during class as Anne describes in her diary. Perhaps it attracted attention over at the Lyceum, but here in the Montessori school they had no reason to be talking. We don't require the children to sit still. They can walk about during class. We don't have order and opposition to it here – we simply reckon the opposition as part of the order.

"When the war came, we were terribly anxious about our school. But it first seemed as though we would come off tolerably well. Once some German officers came who wanted to requisition the school building, but when they saw that we had no central heating they left again. Everything went on as before, and in fact the last year was particularly nice. We had started to do theatricals. The children wrote the plays in one class, and in the following class we put them on. Anne was in her element. Of course she was full of ideas for the scripts, but since she also had no shyness and liked imitating other people, the big parts fell to her. She was rather small among her schoolmates, but when she played the queen or the princess she suddenly seemed a good bit taller than the others. It was really strange to see that.

"And in the middle of this lovely year came the decree. The children had to be separated. We were forced to let eighty-seven pupils go. It was not until this happened that we realized how many Jewish children we had had. Eighty-seven. In Anne's class alone there were twenty…"

And Mrs K took up the class rolls once more and showed me the red marks. Eighty-seven names were crossed out in red.

"For a while we saw her again quite often. But then they were suddenly all wearing the yellow stars, and then we no longer saw them at all. After the war, only twenty came back. Twenty out of eighty-seven.

"But if you want to know what sort of things Anne did here in school, you need only go through the class. Don't be afraid of disturbing the children. Look at anything you like."

So I went around the class. I stood for a moment beside two boys who were busy with a plastic model of North America. One of them had a tiny flag labelled "Chicago" and together we tried to find the hole where this flag should go. Suddenly Mrs K came up behind me, drew me slightly to one side and said to me:

"Look over there…"

In the corner sat a small blonde girl, reading, head propped in her hands. You could tell that nothing, nothing, not even a cannon shot, could have torn her away from her book.

Mrs K whispered: "That is how you must picture Anne, just like that.

59

"Not blonde, of course, but she just looked like that. That was her seat too."

In turning a page the girl raised her head a little and glanced towards us, but there was no danger of her realising we were watching her, for what she wanted to see was already there, inside her eyes. I heard Mrs K saying:

"I'm very fond of her. Of course a teacher must not play favourites, but there are simply children who do not seem strangers to one for a single moment.

"Anne was such a child too."

CHAPTER 4

Ten Seconds

The wedding guests have driven up. They leave their cabs, greet one another on the pavement, and give us friendly smiles, but they seem to be looking towards us from a great distance – for some of them are by now already dead, says Dr K, who is running the projector. Uncle Frans, for example, the gentleman in the centre, and the lady at the extreme right are no longer among the living. But you cannot see by the look of people whether they are destined to die or live. They smile awkwardly and walk stiffly towards the front door of the house, where the gentlemen allow the ladies to precede them and the door finally closes behind the last guest. And for a moment it seems as if we are witnessing a trick film, or something conceived by Chaplin: the door springs open again immediately, and the people reappear. But they all seem transformed. It is as if they had entered the house only in order to don other faces hastily, for now they are laughing and talking, are in the highest spirits, and behind them the newly-weds appear on the steps, Dr K in morning dress and top hat, and his bride, who is now his wife and sits beside him, in a white gown. They come down the steps, and the chauffeurs touch their caps, and all drive away.

For just a moment the camera seems uncertain where to look. It darts to the right, then to the left, then whisks up the wall of the house along the ripple of bright Dutch tiles, and into view comes a window crowded with people who are waving after the departing cars. The camera swings farther, to the left now, past an empty window and to the third on the floor. There a girl stands alone, looking out into space. But

61

just as the man on the street, the man with the camera, is about to pass on, the child moves her head a trifle, so that her face can be seen. The camera pauses, and her face flits more into focus; her hair sways lightly and shimmers from the sun. And at this moment she discovers the camera, discovers the man on the street, discovers us, and laughs, laughs at us, laughs with sudden merriment and surprise and embarrassment all at the same time, laughs as one does upon celluloid film and across the span of sixteen years when one is no cinema star. There is a touch of coquetry and of hope; she lifts her head and throws it back, and her mouth moves, calling out something no one can now hear; she calls over her shoulder into the room, and her hand moves to beckon to the window someone inside the room. But at this moment the ten seconds are over, ten of the 500 million seconds that were the duration of Anne's life. The film is over. Her laugh breaks off. The nearness, the shadow of truth, vanishes. The white screen becomes cold and vacant. Mrs K stands up, goes to the door, and switches on the light.

As Dr K lets the reel rewind so that he can show it a second time, he explains how the picture happened to have been taken. He himself did not know Anne at all, and his wife knew her only from Anne's girlhood days on Merwedeplein, simply as one knows the children of neighbours, from seeing them on the street and greeting them in the early morning. The friend who had filmed their wedding also did not know Anne, and the doctor guesses that there was a small strip of film left on the reel, not enough to do anything with, and so his friend had simply taken a shot into the blue. He had certainly never imagined that out of the blue he would catch in his lens ten seconds of history.

*

So that was Anne, for ten seconds. Had she known who she was? I turn over this question, but there is no answer. Certainly there is no doubt that she tried to find out. I have seen many snapshots of her, kept by her friends. Mr Frank also showed me the photograph album which Mrs Frank started when she was a baby. And Anne also collected pictures of herself, and sometimes wrote little comments in the margin:

What a joke!
Now what's coming?
I'm fine.
Not bad either.
I wish I'd always look like this. Then I'd have a chance for Hollywood. But at the moment unfortunately I usually look different.

The best picture of all is the last one taken of her. Anne is sitting at a table, over a book or notebook, arms laid one upon the other. She is wearing a white lace blouse. Her hair is long and loose, and she is smiling. But above all her mouth is smiling; there is not much smile in her eyes. They are large eyes, and there is a certain heaviness in their gaze; not melancholy, but it is as if they were heavy with experiences that go far beyond her own limited scope.

Anne once drew up a list to which she gave the heading: 'Beauty'. She enumerated what she thought to be the characteristics of a beautiful woman, then checked over her own qualities to determine in what degree she met these standards. This is the list:

Black hair and blue eyes?	*No*
Dimples in the cheeks?	*Yes*
Dimple in the chin?	*Yes*

Good complexion?	*Yes*
Small mouth?	*No*
Nice fingernails?	*Sometimes*
Intelligent?	*Sometimes*

She had no illusions about how she would make out in Hollywood with such a score. In one of her notebooks I found a long and quite surprising story. It is surprising first of all because it consists purely and simply of a teenager's wish-dream. The narration is better than most teenagers would manage, but still it remains a teenage dream. The end of the story, however, is surprising in a different fashion.

The story was written in December 1943, when she had already been imprisoned in her hiding-place for eighteen months. The tale begins with the heroine, who calls herself 'Anne Franklin', writing a letter to two American film actresses, two youthful sisters whose devoted fan she has been. The sisters answer, a correspondence develops, and one day the Lane sisters invite her to come to California for the school holiday. Anne's parents give her permission to go. The girls have a glorious time on the beaches of the Pacific Coast, and one day Priscilla Lane suddenly asks our Anne whether she would not like to be a film star herself. Anne says yes.

I must admit that I had seen this coming, and I read on with some trepidation. But my anxiety was needless, as I should have realised earlier, for the seaside life on the Pacific was described in terms altogether different from the usual clichés. All is gay and simple, in no way like life in a movie colony; rather, the beach and its pleasures are much like those of Scheveningen, an hour from Amsterdam, although perhaps the sun shines somewhat more warmly. At any rate, Anne is ready to start on her actress career…

... And so next day I really went to one of those offices. There was a terrible bustle, and lots of girls were already waiting in line at the door... I waited two hours, and then my turn came. A little bell rang, and I walked bravely into the office where a middle-aged man sat behind a desk. He greeted me rather coldly, asked my name and address, and was greatly astonished when he heard that I was staying with the Lanes. After the questioning was over, he looked closely at me once more and asked:

'So you really want to be a film star?'

And I answered:

'Very much so, sir, if I'm suited for it.'

He pressed a buzzer and immediately a smartly dressed secretary came in and asked me to follow her...

Anne was given a screen test, and then she went home. A week later the middle-aged gentleman informed her that the pictures had turned out very nicely and inquired whether she would model for a tennis-racket manufacturer. Anne accepted with alacrity...

... The following day I went to the photographer's studio. Thereafter I had to go there every day for a week. I changed clothes, had to stand and sit and smile all the time; then again I had to run and change my clothes again, look charming and make up my face. At night I was so tired that I could barely drag myself to bed. After three days I could scarcely manage to smile any more, but I had to keep my agreement. And when I came home to the Lanes on the fourth evening, I looked so pale that Mrs Lane simply forbade me to pose again... and I was heartily grateful to her for that. I was cured forever of my illusions of fame, and was able to enjoy my vacation again...

Mrs K switched off the light again, and once more the room darkened and the wall brightened, and Anne laughed at us again. But when Dr K started the film for the third time, recapitulating the snatch out of the blue, the evocation of ten vanished seconds – when Anne turned her head again, and again looked surprised and laughed – Dr K stopped the projector, so that her smile froze and we could stand up and examine Anne's face closely. The smile stood still, a hand's breadth above our heads; it was no longer alive, and when I walked forward so close to the screen that I could have touched it, it ceased to be a smile, ceased even to be a face, for the canvas was granular and the beam of light split into a multitude of tiny shadows, as if it were scattered upon a sandy plain.

CHAPTER 5

Deadlines and Top-Secret Orders

Frau Lotte Düssel: "We lived in Berlin. My husband was Jewish; I am a Catholic. We would speak about the matter when speaking made us feel better, and we would say nothing about it when silence made us feel better.

"On Friday evenings my husband would sometimes say to me: 'Look outside, Lotte, and see whether a star is visible yet.' When the star appeared, his Sabbath began. Nowadays I sometimes think that those twenty-four hours every week were what kept us so close to one another.

"He left Berlin after the terrible night in November 1938 and emigrated to Holland. But many of the Dutch did not believe the stories we told them about Germany. Not even the Jews in Holland could believe it."

FROM THE CALENDAR OF HELL

May 10, 1940: 'Operation Yellow'. The German Army invades the Netherlands.

May 14–15, 1940: Capitulation of the Netherlands.

STATEMENTS

From the diary of a reserve lieutenant in the Dutch artillery corps, May 10, 1940[1]:

"The telephone from Nijdam reports: A tank column... passing through... violent fire... stops a little behind our front...

"Telephone: German infantry leaving the tanks... violent

---

[1] From the anthology *Dagboekfragmenten 1940–1945* (Martinus Nijhoff, the Hague, 1954).

fire… our own infantry is taken completely by surprise…

"The report breaks off. I stay at the phone, calling: 'Nijdam! Nijdam!'"

Frau Lotte Düssel says: "We did not notice much in Amsterdam. The firing was very far away. There were only the planes overhead, and the searchlights at night. And people were saying: 'They are dropping down everywhere with parachutes.'"

From the diary of a Dutch Nazi, an inspector of police who had been arrested at the beginning of hostilities[2]:

"It had come at last. We were free again, and with heads high we stood before the hangdog gang at police headquarters. We were given back our badges, and I drove the chief inspector's car home. What a reunion! So moving, to see Marie and the children again. Kloos and Jet, Piet Sikkens and Agnes, his wife, came over too. Wonderful, wonderful – the ordeal is over. Our day is coming."

Otto Frank says: "It was very quiet in Amsterdam. But at the beginning of June I once saw a German Army car coming down Scheldestraat and turning into Norder-Amstellaan. At the corner it stopped and the driver asked the flower-seller, who had his stand there, some question. Then they drove on. But at the next corner the car turned around, returned, stopped again at the Scheldestraat corner, and a soldier jumped out and slapped the flower-seller's face. That was how it began."

FROM THE CALENDAR OF HELL

July 2, 1940: *The Verondnungsblatt des Reichkomissars für die Besetzten Niederlande (Official Gazette of the Reich Commissioner*

[2] *Ibid.*

for the Occupied Netherlands) announces the following decree: "All Jews of other than Dutch nationality are required to report at once…"

STATEMENT

Frau Lotte Düssel: "My husband stopped coming home at night; he slept at the homes of acquaintances. Of course he did not report. Someone in the Dutch Alien Office telephoned a warning to us. And at six o'clock in the morning – I had heard the sounds of cars in front of the house, and the ringing of the bell and the voice of our landlady, but I was so sleepy that I did not wake up until he stood before me.

"These movies and the caricatures we see in the newspapers nowadays are all wrong. Their appearance was quite different. When I looked up from my bed, I saw a blond young man with a boyish face and a death's-head on his cap. He spoke quite reasonably, even a little uncertainly, the way boys do talk. But when I looked down – those riding breeches! And how squarely he stood there with legs wide apart! And his boots, and his fists resting on his hips…

"He left again. He was not looking for my husband at all, but for a Social Democratic deputy who had once lived in our house. We really did not know where he was hiding now."

FROM THE CALENDAR OF HELL

October 22, 1940: The *Official Gazette* announced that all industrial or commercial firms owned by Jews or having Jewish partners are to be reported. Infractions of this order will be punished by up to five years' imprisonment or fines of up to 100,000 gulden, 'in so far as such acts are not liable to heavier penalties under regulations'.

November 25, 1940: Dismissal of Jews from all Governmental and public offices.

January 9, 1941: The Dutch Association of Theatre Managers is instructed to forbid Jews entry into cinemas at all times.

January 10, 1941: All persons of the Jewish religion, or wholly or partly of Jewish blood, 'are to report'. Failure to report will be considered a crime.

February 11, 1941: Jewish students are forbidden to matriculate in any Dutch university. Students already matriculated require special permission to continue their studies.

February 22–25, 1941: First round-up of Jews in Amsterdam.

June 4, 1941: Jews are forbidden to visit bathhouses or public parks.

June 11, 1941: More round-ups.

October 22, 1941: The Reich Commissioner issues a decree under which Jews can be forbidden to hold jobs. Jews employed by a single firm for ten years are to receive one-and-a-half month's pay when dismissed.

December 5, 1941: All non-Dutch Jews are to report for 'voluntary emigration'.

December 28, 1941: A secret balance sheet for the first year of occupation, found among the documents of the Chief of the SS and Secret Police in the Netherlands, lists:

Hostages currently on hand	238
Arrestees awaiting criminal trial	1,433
Jews delivered to reception camp	1,354
Survivors of 900 Jews deported to Mauthausen in the course of the year	8
	3,033

Nine months after this sum was done:

by Chief of the SS and Secret Police in the Occupied Netherlands, to Heinrich Himmler:

Reichsführer:

I take the liberty of placing before you an interim report on the deportation of the Jews. Up to the present, including the Jews deported punitively to Mauthausen, we have started some 20,000 Jews on the way to Auschwitz. In all of Holland approximately 120,000 Jews are to be deported; this figure, however, includes a number of hybrid Jews who, as you know, are to remain here for the present... These will amount to about 6,000 cases, so that approximately 14,000 Jews from mixed marriages will remain here for the present.

In the Netherlands there exists a so-called *Werkverruiming...* a labour scheme whereby Jews are kept at various employments in closed factories and camps. Hitherto we have left these Werkverruiming camps untouched, in order to let the Jews come to them. At present there are about 7,000 Jews in these camps. We hope to reach the figure of 8,000 Jews by October 1. These 8,000 Jews have approximately 22,000 relations in the whole of Holland. On October 1 the Werkverruiming camps will be abruptly taken over by me at one stroke, and on the same day the relations outside the camps will be arrested and taken to the two large, newly established Jew camps at Eesterbork near Assen and Vught near Hertogenbosch. I shall try to obtain three instead of two trains per week. Deportation of these 30,000 Jews will begin from October 1 on. I hope that by Christmas we shall also be rid of these 30,000 Jews, so that altogether 50,000 Jews, that is half the total, will have been removed from Holland...

71

On October 15 the Jews in Holland will be declared outlaws; that is, a large-scale police operation will be set in motion. Not only the German and Dutch police will be enlisted for this, but also the labour groups of the National Socialist Party, the Party branches, the NSB (the Dutch Nazi party), the Army, etc. Every Jew found anywhere in Holland will be delivered to one of the big camps for Jews.

Thereafter no Jew unless specifically exempted will be seen in Holland. Simultaneously I am issuing proclamations declaring that Aryans who have kept Jews hidden, smuggled Jews across the border, or falsified identity papers will have their property confiscated and will themselves be sent to a concentration camp. The purpose of this is to check the flight of the Jews, which has begun on a large scale...

The new Dutch police units are behaving excellently on the Jewish question; day and night they are arresting Jews by the hundred. The only danger involved in this is the fact that here and there a police officer's hand strays and he enriches himself out of Jewish property...

The Jew camp of Westerbork is already completed; the Jew camp of Vught will be finished between October 10th and 15th.

Heil Hitler!
Respectfully yours,
RAUTER.

FROM THE CALENDAR OF HELL

January 17, 1942: Expulsion of the Jews from Zaandam.

April 1, 1942: The Reich Commissioner orders 'the purging of the hospitals of Jewish patients'.

April 29, 1942: Introduction of the star for Jews in the Netherlands.

The form of the Jewish star imposed on the Jews by the Nazis was patterned after the 'yellow patch' customary in some places and at some periods during the Middle Ages. It was a black-bordered, six-pointed star of yellow cloth, the size of the palm of a hand, bearing the word 'JOOD' (Jew) in black, Hebraized letters. The German police set up distribution stations where these stars could be obtained in return for payment of a certain sum and surrender of one stamp from the cloth-ration card.

Every Jew had to wear the yellow star on the left side of his coat and of his outer garments. Jews were also forbidden to appear in the garden, on the balcony, at the door or window of their own homes, without displaying the star.

The Jewish star was introduced into the occupied countries in 1942. In Denmark alone the ordinance had to be withdrawn after King Christian X declared, as soon as the order was publicised, that he himself would be the first to wear the star. But in other occupied countries there were difficulties with the public. These were particularly acute in Paris. The chief of the Paris *Sicherheitsdienst* (the police force of the SS) wrote to the office in The Hague asking for a report on their experiences with the introduction of the star in Holland. Through official channels he received the following confidential reply on June 8th, 1942:

'In hostilely oriented circles, particularly the religious groups, the measure... has evoked antipathy to the Occupying Power and general sympathy for the Jews. The measure was regarded as a new inroad on Dutch sovereignty and the earmarking of the Jews was considered a disgrace to the entire Dutch people. Initially this measure was not approved even in National Socialist circles in Holland. It was frequently observed in public that marked Jews were treated by the Dutch with emphatic politeness. During the early days the Dutch expressed their sympathy for the Jews by themselves wearing genuine or imitated Jewish stars. Energetic measures against these persons, as well as against Jews who wore no star, have pacified the general mood to a certain degree... Members of the Jewish race, who at the beginning wore the star with pride, have meanwhile become somewhat more modest since they are threatened by new measures on the part of the Occupying Power. The Jews who wore no star were arrested without delay. We have requested reception of them in the Mauthausen concentration camp...

'New measures against the Jews are envisioned for this week...

(signed) ZOEPF
SS Hauptsturmführer'

STATEMENTS

Mrs S, who was a child at that time and lived on Merwedeplein in Amsterdam, says:

"My parents allowed me to wear the star a few days before the deadline. As you see, I am blonde, and I thought: if they see you with the star, they'll think that all the Christians are wearing stars too."

From the diary of a Dutch woman of Veluwe[3]:

"May 3, 1942. – Joop went to church this morning with a Jewish star pinned to her chest. In my opinion it is foolhardy to let oneself be locked up for anything like that. It does so little to help, and I am afraid. If everyone did it, it might make an impression, but there are so few after all... It is difficult to say what we should do..."

[3] *Op. cit.*

Dr H relates:

"The first day we had to wear the star was a Saturday. In the afternoon I went to a cafe where we Jews were allowed. I had the star on my coat, but not on my jacket yet. This was true of most of the others in the cafe. It was around half past three when the Gestapo came storming in, twelve men. Everyone screamed. I snatched my coat from the hook, but did not have time to put it on. I draped it around my shoulders. Then they were already standing in front of me, ordering me to come along...

"They led us at the double to the Gestapo headquarters. On the way I threw away my gold watch and my address book, with the addresses of all my friends. Luckily no one saw me.

"In the Gestapo headquarters we had to stand with our faces to the wall, and they strutted up and down behind our backs, talking at us and sometimes bellowing. But their shouts did not really sound dangerous. Rather, disgusting.

"After a few hours we were abruptly dismissed, and that same evening we had to return and show that we were also wearing the star on the jackets of our suits.

"That was in April. Soon afterwards I went into hiding."

Madame van der Waal says:

"When it started I told myself: we'll just take Anne to live with us. But my husband was also a Jew, and under supervision, and Jopie also had to wear the star..."

Otto Frank said to me:

"We tried our best to keep these things from obtruding on the children. I had already left my firm at the end of 1941. Previously I had tried to persuade the German affiliate of our company, Travis, Inc., to help us. They behaved quite decently, but it was no longer of any use. I withdrew, and Mr

Koophuis took over the firm. He had been in business with me for a long time.

"The children were scarcely aware of it when we had to register. I went alone. The Dutch official who was in charge of the list did not say a word when he saw me.

"Naturally the children knew what was going on. After all, they had been forced to change schools, and they could not help hearing the military cars in the streets at night. Besides, they, too, were wearing the star now. But the Dutch were good to us, and there were still so many children wearing the star in the neighbourhood. It was not yet very noticeable that their numbers were diminishing."

Toosje says:

"This was the time when planes were over Amsterdam every night. There was an alarm, and we all stood together under the archway of the wall, at the entrance to the house, we and the Franks and other people from the house, and searchlights were passing across the sky, and the anti-aircraft guns boomed and flashed, and Anne was standing beside me, the star on her breast, and we were all frightened. Anne was terribly frightened. But then there was also a man named Dr Beffie from the house next door. He always came over to join us during an alarm, and every time he had a piece of bread in his hand and would eat it. He chewed slowly, so very slowly, and Anne could not help staring at him, no matter how frightened she was. And once, just as the all-clear came, Anne said to me: 'Good heavens, if I chewed so slowly I think I'd be hungry all my life.'"

Mrs L, Trees's mother, said to me:

"One day Anne and Margot were visiting us and said they might report to the Westerbork work camp. I was terribly upset, and asked: 'Why, what do your parents say about that?'

And I thought to myself: You must talk with the Franks. But Anne reassured me; it wasn't so bad there as I imagined, she said. I went on thinking: You must talk to the Franks at once."

Otto Frank says:

"Once danger came very close. On the street I had run into an acquaintance whose wife sometimes worked for the Travis company. We talked about the war, and the man said: 'It will be over soon.' I asked: 'Do you really believe that?' And he looked at me and said: 'Don't you?'

"That was the whole conversation. I did not like him very much.

"A week later a stranger came to the office to see me. He closed the door behind him and told me his name. He also said bluntly that he worked as a courier between the Dutch Nazis and the Gestapo, and asked me for twenty gulden. I gave them to him, and he handed me a letter, I opened it. It was a report from my acquaintance to the Gestapo, alleging that I had expressed doubt of German victory and had attempted to influence him.

"The stranger said: 'You can keep the letter. Or perhaps you'll do better to tear it up. I took it out of the file of incoming reports.'

"After the war, when I came back from Auschwitz, I looked for the man. He was in prison as a political criminal. I went to the commission and said: 'That man once saved my life.' But they showed me the documents on him, and I saw that I was the only person he had saved. He had betrayed a great many others...

"The man did not know me. And if he had come on account of the twenty gulden – he could have extorted far more than that from me. I cannot understand him, but he saved me. And in Auschwitz, too, I came through, the only one of us. But I do not like to speak of a guardian angel. How could any angel have had the heart to save a man alone, without his family?"

FROM THE CALENDAR OF HELL

June 30, 1942: The Reich Commissioner imposes a curfew upon Jews. They must remain in their homes from 8.00pm to 6.00am, and during this time neither pay nor receive visits and keep the windows of their rooms shut. On public transport lines still open to them they must utilise the smoking-compartments of the lowest-class carriages and remain standing unless all other passengers have already found seats. Jews are furthermore forbidden to have telephones or to make use of public telephone booths. They are not permitted to shop at weekly markets at certain times, and certain quarters of the cities are completely closed to them. Finally, only a limited number of medicines and drugs are to be available for Jews.

From July 14, 1942, on: Continual round-ups of Jews in Amsterdam.

STATEMENTS

"But on Monday morning," says Toosje, "I think it was the sixth… yes, on the sixth of July, at noon, Mr Goudsmit, who lived near the Franks, came to see us and said: 'The Franks are gone.' And he gave my mother a note he had found on the table in the house, and they talked together, and I saw that he had Anne's tomcat in his arms. I took Moortje from him, and he also gave me the plate of meat for the cat, which he had found on the table, and I went to the kitchen and fed Moortje. After a while my mother came into the kitchen. She watched Moortje eating, and said to me: 'We'll keep him here.'"

Madame van der Waal says:

"When we heard that the Franks were gone – to Switzerland, so we were told; a German Army officer whom Mr Frank had known in the first war was supposed to have taken them there – we were all glad, everyone I know. A few days later Jopie and Lies went up to the Franks' flat because they wanted to see whether they could find anything of Anne's. They did find her swimming medals and took them home."

Around this same time Anne wrote a farewell letter to Jopie – this was when Anne was already in the hideout. I found the letter among her papers. She wrote that Jopie need not worry; all was well with her. And the same day she wrote a second letter to Jopie, pretending that Jopie had answered hers, for she wrote:

I was so awfully glad to get your letter...

And she asked Jopie to tear her letters into little pieces so that no one would find them and discover where she was hiding...

Of course none of Anne's letters ever reached anyone, including Jopie. Anne knew that perfectly well. She did not even attempt to mail them, but kept them all in her notebook. But it was as though life, 'normal life', continued on for a little while, just as the heart of some animals will go on twitching for a while after death.

Mrs C says:

"I emigrated to Holland in 1933. Here I worked in a bookshop, and from 1942 on I stayed in hiding, sometimes in one place, sometimes in another. I spent the longest period in a shelter for the homeless.

"I saw Anne's play when it was given in Amsterdam, and two moments in it almost choked me: the Hanukkah celebration and the moment when Peter and Anne talk about the yellow stars on their clothes. The one reminded me of my childhood, the other of the end of all innocence."

CHAPTER 6

The Walk in the Rain

Of all the great coastal cities of the world, Amsterdam has been won from the sea by the greatest effort. It leans its brow against the Ij, an arm of the sea lined with piers and warehouses, where ocean liners dock. A river winds through the city, and half a hundred canals in which the brackish water lies mute, lurking, fermenting, a malignant black sheen upon its surface.

The Old City is stitched together by hundreds of bridges large and small. Along the paved banks of the canals stand linden and elm trees, and behind these the narrow, tall-windowed houses of dark Dutch bricks, topped by steeples and sawtooth gables, and the shifting, inconstant light from the sea. And over all stretches the moodiest of skies, lighter and faster-moving, but also heavier and more portentous than the sky anywhere else in the world.

During my stay in the city, the weather changed. The hotel porter said: "Now we're going to have real Amsterdam weather."

So we did. It poured for a full week. On the last day I climbed up to the Westertoren. From the tower the sky was like one vast swell of the sea. Rain poured out of flying cloud fronts; then came light; then more clouds and shafts of rain, and more light in the distance. The light and the shafts of rain looped and swooped over the city, and among them a few gulls flashed like white sparks. The streets and roofs were steeped in wetness, as if Amsterdam were on the point of sinking into the sea again.

I stood on the south side of the observation gallery that runs around the tower. The wall behind my back protected me slightly from the rain and hail. I was looking for a particular street down there in the city below, but I could not find it among the many that led from the clean, bright suburbs to the dark, intrigue-filled heart of Amsterdam. It must be one of them, I knew, one coming from the southeast. But had they walked along the canal? Or down Vijzelstraat?

Streets are mute.

So we walked in the pouring rain... each with a school satchel and shopping bag filled to the brim with all kinds of things thrown together anyhow. We got sympathetic looks from people on their way to work. You could see by their faces how sorry they were they couldn't offer us a lift; the gaudy yellow star spoke for itself. Only when we were on the road did Mummy and Daddy begin to tell me bits and pieces about the plan... when we arrived at the Prinsengracht, Miep took us quickly upstairs and into the 'Secret Annexe'. She closed the door behind us and we were alone.

So Anne wrote in her diary. But pity and shame could have been felt on any street in this city, and I did not find the particular one, hard as I searched for it.

I walked halfway around the tower, to the north-east corner, and looked down Prinsengracht. I could see the house. It stands on the bank of the canal, about a hundred or a hundred and fifty yards from the tower. The Secret Annexe is roofed with black-painted tin or asphalt roofing paper, and in the yard, in front of Anne's and Peter's window, stands the huge chestnut tree, its wind-tossed top rising higher than the building itself.

From my favourite spot on the floor I look up at the blue sky and the bare chestnut tree, on whose branches little raindrops shine, appearing like silver, and at the seagulls...

The Walk in the Rain

Now the chestnut tree was in full leaf. It looked black, soaked with rain, dripping. The gulls, too, had vanished, retiring all at once before a new cloud front which was now approaching. It came; overhead there was a roar, and hail spat greyly down out of the streaming cloud. A veil of grey was suddenly drawn over the canal. For a moment the house and the black tree could still be seen dimly, as through hammered glass. Then they too were gone. The hail clattered against the copper dome of the tower. Something struck my head and lashed into my face, and I took shelter inside the tower.

> *The hiding place...* [is] *in the building where Daddy has his office... Daddy didn't have many people working for him: Mr Kraler, Koophuis, Miep, and Elli Vossen, a twenty-three-year-old typist, who all knew of our arrival. Mr Vossen, Elli's father, and two boys worked in the warehouse; they had not been told.*
> (*Diary*, July 9, 1942)

Mr Vossen died in 1954, Mr Kraler, who after Mr van Daan's withdrawal took over the management of dealings between Travis, Inc. and the affiliated firm of Kohlen & Co., is now living in Canada. He has corresponded with me. But Miep, Elli, and Mr Koophuis I spoke to personally.

I confess I felt strange to be sitting opposite them. I knew them, after all, from reading the *Diary* and seeing them on the stage. In the stage version of the *Diary* Elli and Miep have been merged into a single person called 'Miep', and Kraler and Koophuis into one called 'Kraler'. But here, in reality, they separated from one another again, and I saw them as living persons.

I do not know how many persons there are in any era whose fate it is to see themselves and their actions upon the stage; but surely there cannot be more than a few dozen, and here were three of them. Elli, Miep, and Koophuis had seen themselves in the theatre, but they were entirely unharmed by the experience. Miep is a small, delicate, intelligent, still young woman; Elli a blooming young Dutch mother such as the old Dutch masters have painted; Koophuis a medium-sized, extremely gaunt man, in poor health, spindly, white-haired. He has a sharp, birdlike face. He looks like anything but a hero, far more a bureaucrat. But he was heroic – heroic out of a sense of order.

Mr Koophuis has known Mr Frank since 1923. They had met on business dealings in Amsterdam. Otto Frank would be coming from Berlin or Frankfurt; he was always going from one place to another. Koophuis describes him as lively and full of energy. He would appear in Amsterdam, and then by the next day he would be gone again.

"Then, in 1933, he suddenly appeared at the door again, and that was the beginning of our long, unreserved friendship," Mr Koophuis says. "We were personal friends, too, but I suppose that does not particularly interest you."

In 1941 Koophuis took over Frank's place in the Travis company; otherwise the firm would have been confiscated or liquidated as a Jewish business. When the round-ups began the following year, Frank often slept at the home of a Travis agent, or in the homes of other acquaintances. In those days he, like many other exiles from Germany, still received warnings from various officials in the Dutch police when danger threatened his quarter of town. A total stranger would suddenly telephone the Franks, say something, and hang up immediately. Naturally, only coded warnings were possible, since telephones could be tapped by the Gestapo.

The situation being what it was, Koophuis and Kraler advised Mr Frank and Mr van Daan, who was in similar peril, that the time had come to look about for a hiding place, in case the persecution grew worse. They proposed the rear

84

building of their place of business on the Prinsengracht, since these rooms were used only occasionally as a laboratory and for storing office files. Laboratory work was no longer carried on, since nowadays they had no choice in raw materials; they poured into the spice mills on the ground floor whatever they were lucky enough to be assigned by the Government economic boards.

The proposal seemed a good one to Frank and van Daan. But since Jews were forbidden to move or even to transport household goods through the street, they gradually had pieces of furniture, rugs, and other necessities removed from their homes, supposedly for cleaning and repairs. Actually, these articles were all taken to Koophuis's home and from there, when occasion offered on a Saturday evening after working hours, moved to the Prinsengracht and hidden in the Secret Annexe.

Miep says:

"Mr Frank bowed to necessity. He resigned from the firm when the time came; he wore the star; he said nothing. He never showed his feelings. I can still see him as he came into the office one day, in his raincoat, and when he unbuttoned the raincoat I saw the star on his chest underneath it. I don't think he had one on the coat. We made an effort to talk with him and act towards him as we always had in the past, and as though it were perfectly natural for him to come to the office now, for we knew that he dreaded pity. It was his way to come to terms with his feelings silently. A very Prussian trait, really."

Elli, the youngest member of the firm, had not noticed the mysterious changes and preparations in the building. She may have seen furniture being brought in and carried up, but she did not put two and two together, and she asked no questions.

During the first week of July, however, all the employees had a meeting in what had formerly been Mr Frank's private office. Mr Frank sat at his desk as he had in the past, and Mr Koophuis told them the whole story. All promised to keep the secret. But none of them suspected that the move would take place that same week.

Mr Koophuis says:

"They telephoned me Sunday afternoon, and that evening I went out to their home on Merwedeplein. A postcard had come ordering Margot to report on Monday to the reception centre for the Westerbork camp. So we said to ourselves: now there is no point in waiting any longer."

Mr Frank says:

"We knew that they sent out these cards, and many people had obeyed the order. It was said that life in the camps, even in the camps in Poland, was not so bad; that the work was hard, but there was food enough, and the persecutions stopped, which was the main thing. I told a great many people what I suspected. I also told them what I had heard on the British radio, but a good many still thought these were atrocity stories. I remember that one day a girl came to say goodbye to us, the daughter of friends, and she told us that she had packed her sketchbook into her rucksack. She was very good at drawing, and she said she wanted to have a few mementos, for later…"

Number 263 Prinsengracht is a tall, narrow old Dutch brick building. Its windows are now blank and empty, for it is no longer occupied. Someone had chalked a few illegible words on the door. Bicycles lean against the wall. One of the lower panels in the door to the warehouse has been repaired at some time. The old panel was smashed in by burglars on April 9th, 1944.

The front of the building has that quiet beauty which can be observed in so many of these old houses in Amsterdam. It comes from the perfect simplicity and the finely balanced proportions.

Apart from the door to the warehouse, the building has two narrow entrances. One of these, which was usually kept closed even when Frank still worked in the firm, leads to a small staircase which goes straight up to the second storey, as is frequently the case in Dutch buildings. It is a steep, dangerous staircase. Behind the other door is a side entrance to the warehouse, and an ordinary staircase.

There is another door at the top of the stairs, with a frosted glass window in it, which has 'Office' written in black letters across it.

The word can still be read.

That is the large main office, very big, very light, and very full. Elli, Miep, and Mr Koophuis work there in the daytime.

The room is empty now, and seems almost a small public hall. The big windows of the façade are almost opaque with dust. The water of the canal and the trees are seen as through a gauze veil.

A small dark room… leads to a small somewhat dark second office. Mr Kraler and Mr Van Daan used to sit here, now it is only Mr Kraler…
From Kraler's office a long passage goes… up four steps and leads to the showroom of the whole building: the private office.

The paint is flaking from the ceiling; strips of wallpaper hang from the walls. The window is heavily shadowed by the chestnut tree in the courtyard.

A wooden staircase leads from the downstairs passage to... a small landing at the top... The right-hand door leads to our 'Secret Annexe'. No one would ever guess...

The cupboard that was built against the door to disguise it has been pulled down. Nothing is left but the twisted hinges hanging beside the door.

I went through the door and turned left, into the Franks' room. It is a low-ceilinged room, empty, like the entire house. It smells of mice and of ten years' silence and neglect. Next to it, on the right, is the tiny, single-windowed room in which Anne and Mr van Düssel lived. Along the wall on the right, where Anne slept, a withered bouquet of flowers lies on the floor. The superintendent told me that schoolchildren from Hamburg had paid the place a visit. A tattered, yellowed remnant of curtain still hangs at the window. Through the curtain the chestnut and the houses across the courtyard appear as in a dream – as it is shortly before awakening, when the dream begins to fade. But from outside this curtain was opaque and no doubt afforded good protection during the day. As I went out I saw, right beside the door of Anne's room, a pencil mark on the torn wallpaper. Next to it is written: 'A 42'.

Mr Frank used to measure his daughters, but the other marks have been stripped off along with the wallpaper. Only this one is left. In 1942 Anne reached exactly to the tip of my nose. Later I measured the height on myself. Two years before the arrest she was about five feet two inches in height.

The van Daans' room on the next floor is large and handsome. The view from the window here extends uninterrupted far out beyond the yard.

In Anne's papers I found a description of Peter's room, which adjoined the van Daans'. She called it *My First Interview*.

The Walk in the Rain

My First Interview

*I hit on the idea of interviewing someone, and since all the persons
in the house have already been thoroughly described, I thought of
Peter, who always keeps in the background...*

*When you knock on the door of his room toward evening, and
hear his soft 'Yes, yes', and then the door opens, you can be sure that
he is peering at you between the top steps of the attic stairs. And he
says, usually with a little note of invitation, 'Well...'*

*His room is – now what is it really? A kind of partitioned-off
garret space, I think, very small, dark and damp. But he had made
a regular room out of it. When he sits to the left of the stairs, there is
certainly no more than a yard between him and the wall. There his
little table stands... and on the other side of the stairs his bike hangs
from the ceiling. This bicycle, at the moment out of commission, is
swathed in wrapping paper...*

*I am still standing in the doorway, now looking at the other side
of the room. Behind the table stands... a sofa upholstered with a blue
floral print; on the arm the fabric has been mended. Above this hangs
a lamp, below that a mirror, and a short distance farther along the
wall is a bookcase which in a really messy boy's way is crammed full
of books covered with wrapping paper. To add to the beautiful effect
(or because the owner could find no other place to wedge it) there is
a wooden box in which you can find anything you're looking for.
It's some time ago, but it really did happen that one day I found in
the depths of this my favourite knife, and that was not the only thing
that came to light.*

*Next to the bookcase is a shelf... which was once intended for milk
bottles and other kitchen things, but since the young occupant's
hoard of books has so greatly increased... the various milk bottles
have now been demoted to the floor.*

*The floor, too... is worth noticing. Not only has he in his room two
large and one small genuine Persian rugs; their colours are also so
glowing that anyone entering the room is immediately struck by them.
The floor, which shakes somewhat and is uneven, so that it must be*

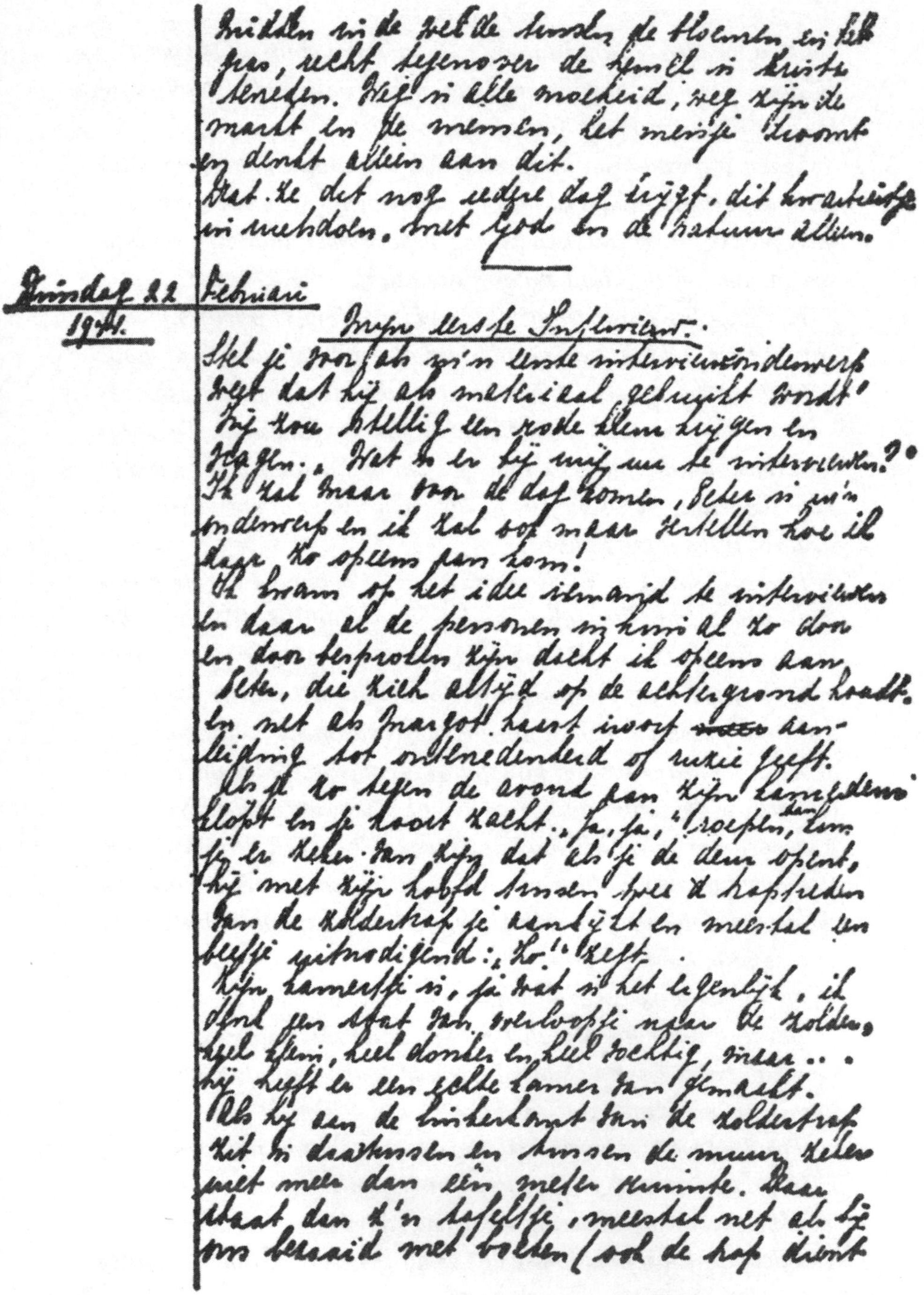

midden in de wereld tussen de bloemen en het gras, recht tegenover de hemel [illegible] tenen. Weg is alle moeheid, weg zijn de markt en de mensen, het meisje droomt en denkt alleen aan dit.
Dat ze dit nog iedere dag krijgt. dit krachtiger [illegible] meedelen. met God en de natuur alleen.

Dinsdag 22 Februari 1944.

Mijn eerste Interview.

Stel je voor dat zo'n eerste interviewonderwerp weet dat hij als materiaal gebruikt wordt! Hij zou stellig een rode kleur krijgen en vragen: „Wat is er bij mij nu te interviewen?" Ik zal maar voor de dag komen, Peter is mijn onderwerp en ik zal nu maar vertellen hoe ik daar zo opeens aan kom!
Ik kwam op het idee iemand te interviewen en daar al de personen in huis al zo door en door besproken zijn dacht ik opeens aan Peter, die zich altijd op de achtergrond houdt. en net als Margot heel weinig ~~[illegible]~~ aanleiding tot ontevredenheid of ruzie geeft.
Als je zo tegen de avond aan zijn kamerdeur klopt en je hoort zacht „Ja, ja," roepen, dan zul je zeker zien dat als je de deur opent, hij met zijn hoofd tussen twee der trapteden van de zoldertrap je aankijkt en meestal een beetje uitnodigend: „Kom!" zegt.
Zijn kamertje is, ja wat is het eigenlijk, ik denk een soort van overloopje naar de zolder, heel klein, heel donker en heel vochtig, maar...
hij heeft er een echte kamer van gemaakt.
Als hij aan de linkerkant van de zoldertrap zit is daar tussen en tussen de muur zeker niet meer dan een meter ruimte. Daar staat dan z'n tafeltje, meestal net als bij ons bezaaid met boeken (ook de trap dient

From Anne's notebook: *My First Interview*

stepped on with care, is covered with these once so precious articles.
Two walls have green burlap stretched over them; the other two walls
are pasted all over with beautiful and not so beautiful movie stars
and advertising posters.

About Peter himself, my opinion has changed a great deal lately.
I used to think him stupid and dull, but now he is neither, just very
nice. I am firmly convinced that he is honest and generous. He
always was modest and helpful, and I have the feeling that he is
much more sensitive than people think... He is certainly not dumb,
and I notice particularly that he has an excellent memory.

I don't need to tell anyone that he is handsome, because anyone
who sees him realizes that. His hair is terrific, a dense brown forest
of curls, blue-grey eyes... After the war I'll paste him in with the
pictures of the others...

I have seen a photograph of Peter. Anne's description is
perfectly accurate. It is, in fact, sharper than any photograph
could be; hence I assume that the description of his room is
also accurate. Now 'the young occupant's' rugs, bookcases,
and books have vanished. The room is once again a
partitioned-off garret space.

The stairs lead up to the attic, which has two small
windows. By leaning out of one of them you can see the
Westertoren, and the golden crown that tops it, with the
silvery-grey dome showing red through slits, and the golden
cross above that, and through the other window the crown
of the big chestnut tree can be seen.

The loft window is always kept open at night now. In the evenings
Peter and I often sit up there... We are having a superb spring
after our long, lingering winter... Our chestnut tree is already
quite greenish and you can even see little blooms here and there.

Now, in June, the blossoms of the chestnut have long since
faded. Standing at this window, I look out upon its greenish-

black foliage. One can see that this tree has been loved. But the sky above it is blank. Or are there tracks in the sands of the sky, only invisible?

From the attic the windows of the houses across the courtyard can be seen. One of these must have contained the apartment of the dentist whom Anne watched attending the teeth of *an old lady, who was awfully scared.* And on the right side of the yard, not thirty yards away, you look into the back window of a house in which Descartes once lived – the philosopher who declared: 'I think, therefore I am.' From this very house he wrote to Jean Louis de Balzac, a friend in France: 'Is there any other country in which one can enjoy freedom as enormously as one does here?'

The sentence is inscribed above the door of the house.

But the Prinsengracht house has no inscription on the door apart from the number. Nevertheless, a girl from Japan wrote to Otto Frank that her heart was in that house.

CHAPTER 7

Marginal Notes

Anne's diary accounts fully for the twenty-five months the
Franks and their friends spent hidden in the Secret Annexe.
Only marginal notes can be added to her chronicle. These
do not make the picture any clearer than it already is, but
they show the frame.

Eight persons lived there illegally. Or, rather, they lived,
but life was illegal. Fate had excluded these eight persons
from the world and from freedom. Or shall I say that we
Germans were in prison, in so far as one child among them
took with her all freedom of the mind? However that may
be, a disguised door separated these eight from the rest of us
for two years. Only a few persons knew the secret lock to that
door.

Mr Koophuis and Mr Kraler had many cares during those
years. The very existence of their two companies was
constantly endangered, because these had formerly been
Jewish firms. The secret of the house converted this danger
into a personal danger to all of them. Moreover, the owner
of the warehouse, Mr Vossen, who was Elli's father, soon fell
ill; he suffered from cancer of the stomach. A new man had
to be hired. His name was M. From the first he behaved in a
pushing, crafty, and unpleasant manner. Now, added to all of
Koophuis's and Kraler's old troubles, was this new one: there
were some persons in the building who knew the secret, and
others from whom it had to be kept. Incidents occurred that
in normal circumstances would not have been worth
mentioning, but that in the given situation led each time to
the brink of disaster. For example, one day a storm damaged

the roof over the Secret Annexe. It had to be repaired. But the man dealing with it would be separated from the group in hiding by only a thin layer of boards. If one of those boards should break… Mr Koophuis's brother, who was a building contractor, helped them out of this difficulty.

Then the owner of the building, which the firm was only renting, decided to sell the property. He appeared with a prospective buyer, and Koophuis had to lead the visitor from floor to floor. Elli believes she recalls that the man who was interested in the house intermixed German with Dutch.

Koophuis showed them the storerooms and offices, but told them he could not take them to the rear of the building (the Secret Annexe) because he had unfortunately mislaid the key. There were a few more rooms there, he said, but nothing in particular to see. The visitors declared themselves satisfied, and left.

Sometimes, too, Mr van Daan telephoned him at night to say they thought they heard burglars, and once there was an actual burglary. But all of them were far less afraid of burglars than of the police.

Mr Koophuis summed it all up by saying it was just something one had to live through, and that luckily he had a wife who had not once complained about it all. She worried only about his health.

The most difficult problem of all was supplying the group in hiding with food. There were, after all, seven persons, and eight from November 1942 on. Ration cards were bought on the black market. Strangers co-operated without so much as asking whom the food was destined for. Some of these had known the Franks. Possibly they suspected Koophuis's secret. But they never asked an embarrassing question. A great many secrets were well kept in those days, Mr Koophuis said.

Eight persons need a great deal of bread. Koophuis went to an Amsterdam baker whom he knew casually. Neither the

Franks nor the van Daans had ever had any contact with the man. Koophuis told the baker that he needed large extra quantities of bread. The baker pretended that he had not heard the damning words, but provided Koophuis with bread for months and months, setting up a kind of charge account for the missing ration stamps.

Later, when Koophuis was released from prison and looked up the baker, to talk over his debts, it turned out that the account amounted to four hundred bread-ration stamps. A bread stamp bought on the black market cost at the time forty gulden. Mr Koophuis said he did not have that much money. Without a word, the baker drew a line through the account.

Miep and her husband, Henk, obtained potatoes and vegetables from *our greengrocer at the corner*, as Anne wrote. And another time she wrote:

This morning our vegetable man was picked up…

I visited the vegetable man, Mr van H. He was seated at the living-room table in his home in Amsterdam-West – a friendly, great-souled man. His wife prepared coffee for us. He no longer had his store on Leliegracht, he told me; he is now living on a pension.

Mr van H is a big, powerful man, in his fifties, I should judge, with big hands and a powerful head: a peasant living in the city.

Though he operated the store on the corner during the war, he spent most of his time going about with a handcart full of vegetables. Every morning a list of addresses was slipped to him, and he delivered the vegetables at those addresses. He never saw any of the recipients. Either he placed the bags outside the door or someone appeared from inside the house to take them from him. Never did he show any curiosity about such transactions. What mattered to him was that people who needed them had something to eat.

He knew Miep, of course, but he never asked how she and her husband could possibly eat such quantities of vegetables. In those days one did not ask any unnecessary questions. Besides, what was there to ask? He did not know the Franks at all. Moreover, he had problems of his own, for he and his wife had also had a Jew concealed in their apartment. They managed all right until April 1944, when someone denounced him and the hundred and five of his friends who had formed a group to provide for and protect those who had gone into hiding.

Sometimes, too, the group had pasted posters on walls at night. Mr van H took from his wallet a snapshot of a wall covered with posters, one advertising the Cologne Fair of 1941, another a photographic contest for German soldiers, and another calling on men to enter the Dutch 'Labour Front'. In the centre is a large poster bearing the word VIKTORIA! The two arms of the V are holding Hitler's head in a tight vice.

They were all denounced, all hundred and five of them, and Mr Weiss as well, whom the vegetable man had hidden in his home. They were taken to the Gestapo prison, then to Camp Vught, then to Oranienburg, then to Gross-Rosen, then to Dora, near Nordhausen, then to Winsleben am See. They were shifted from concentration camp to concentration camp – but of the 3,000 men who were en route for three and a half days from Gross-Rosen to Dora in thirty cattle trucks 2,700 froze to death. Mr van H was lucky; he returned home after the war. He and four others of the hundred and five.

When I took my leave, he accompanied me, shuffling, to the door. He had both legs frozen on that trip from Gross-Rosen, which is in Silesia, to Dora in the Harz Mountains.

*

Mr Frank said to me that in the early days they had lived in constant terror that the police would find them sooner or later. But as month after month passed, the first year and then the second, and as news came of the invasion and the advance of the Allied troops in France, they began to feel almost lighthearted and quite hopeful. On the other hand, they had a fear of fire breaking out in the Secret Annexe and their being driven into the streets.

The house was old, and there was a good deal of wood in the structure. A moment's carelessness, a single match, would have sufficed to set it ablaze. For that reason they always kept a small number of belongings packed for emergencies. Each one had a knapsack in readiness. Mr Frank himself was also to take, in addition to the knapsack, the briefcase containing Anne's notebooks and diaries. He had promised her that. After all, bombs were falling upon Amsterdam, and night after night squadrons of planes passed over the room. There were dangers enough, and they had no air-raid shelter. Sometimes the house groaned and shook from the salvos of the anti-aircraft batteries.

These nights, he told me, had cost Anne more strength than she really had. Sometimes her nerves would give way completely and she could not grow calmer until he took her into his bed.

Among Anne's stories was one written in such anxiety.

Fear

It was a frightful period I passed through at that time. All around us the war raged, and no one knew whether he would still be alive an hour hence. My parents, brothers and sisters and I lived in the city, but we expected that we would be evacuated or would have to flee. The days were full of firing and the thunder of cannon, the nights full of mysterious sparks and rumbles that seemed to come out of the depths of the earth.

I cannot describe it. In fact, I no longer remember the tumult of those days in detail. I recall only that all day long I did nothing but shake with fear. My parents tried to reassure me in every possible way, but nothing helped. I was frightened, inside and out. I did not eat, slept badly, trembled all the time. For a whole week it went on like that, until a night came that I remember as if it were yesterday.

About half past eight at night, just as the firing was lessening somewhat, I lay fully dressed on the sofa, trying to sleep. Suddenly we were startled by two horrible explosions. As though pricked by needles, we sprang to our feet, all of us at once, and ran out into the hall. Even Mother, who was always so calm, looked deathly pale. The reports were repeated at regular intervals, and suddenly we heard a frightful crash, the sound of shattering glass, and screams, and I ran away as fast as I could. With my knapsack on my back and wearing lots of clothes, I ran away, away from this terrible, burning confusion. All around, everywhere, people were howling and screaming; the street was bright as day from burning houses, and everything looked fearfully burning and red.

I did not think of my parents, my brothers and sisters; I thought only of myself and that I must get away, farther and farther away. I felt no tiredness; my fear was stronger. I did not notice that I had lost my knapsack; I just ran on. I do not know how long any more I ran that way, with the scene of burning houses, screaming people and contorted faces always before my eyes. My fear was everything in the world.

Suddenly I realized that it had become quieter all around me. I looked about as if awakening from a dream, and saw no one, nothing. No fire, no bombs, no people.

I stood still. I was in a meadow. Above my head the stars blazed and the moon shone; the weather was glorious, the night cool but not cold. I no longer heard a sound. Exhausted, I sat down on the ground, spread out the blanket I still had with me, and pillowed my head on it.

I looked up at the sky, and all at once I realized that I was no longer afraid, no longer felt anything at all, that I was quite calm. How crazy that I did not have a thought about my family and even felt no longing for them. I wanted nothing but quiet, and before long I fell asleep right there in the grass under the open sky.

When I awoke, the sun was just rising. I knew at once where I was, for in the distance, bathed in bright light, I saw houses I knew, houses on the outskirts of our city.

I rubbed my eyes and looked around once more. No one was in the vicinity. Only the horsetails and the clover in the grass kept me company. I lay back on my blanket once more and considered what to do now. But my thoughts kept wandering off to the strange feeling that I had had during the night when I sat alone in the grass and was without fear.

Later I found my parents again, and we lived together in another city.

Now that the war is long past, I know how it came about that my fear vanished under the spreading sky. At that time, alone with nature, I understood that fear does not help and is useless. Anyone who is as frightened as I was then will do best to look at nature and to see that God is much closer to us than most people imagine.

Since that time, no matter how many bombs fell close by me thereafter, I never felt real fear again.

This story was written exactly one year before Anne's death. I think that the place from which the *alter ego*, the other Anne of the story, fled was not the Old City, although she had been living in the Prinsengracht house for almost two years. In her nightmare she had been transposed back to Merwedeplein, and, when her house was hit, she chose the route she used to take to the Montessori school, then ran past the school to the end of Niersstraat, where the houses suddenly come to an end and there begins a big, weedy meadow which leads on to the dikes and the Buitenverdertse marsh.

*

Were any of the occupants of the Secret Annexe acquainted with this story?

Mr Frank told me that Anne used to read a page or two from her diary now and then, and sometimes one of her stories, but she had not read this one. Nor, he said, would he have considered it good if too much were publicly said about Anne's writing, because writing is something everyone has to settle with himself.

Mr Kraler in Toronto – whom a Canadian journalist describes as a man of medium height, 'academic in appearance', and looking much younger than his fifty-six years – says nothing at all about Anne's diary or her stories in the long letter he wrote me. In his opinion Anne was not as intelligent as her sister, or at any rate not as mentally developed, but there was something strange about her, something he could almost call wise. He tells the following story:

"My wife and I visited the Franks in their flat on Merwedeplein one last time before they went into hiding. Other friends were present also. During dinner Anne and my wife sat side by side. They talked avidly with one another, for the two got on very well. Then came the soup. Anne was in the midst of telling my wife something. Abruptly she stopped and fell silent, looked into my wife's eyes, and my wife lowered her spoon and looked at Anne, also saying nothing, and there was a long passage of this between the two, of silence and looking at one another, until Anne suddenly looked around at us and said aloud:

" 'Now Mrs Kraler and I have been talking to one another, and nobody heard us.'

"You have no idea," Mr Kraler continues, "of the immense expression of which Anne's eyes were capable. Sometimes it seemed as if she were looking to see whether she had been correctly understood at all. But then again, suddenly and without transition, she could be quite childish. When they were in the Secret Annexe she was always begging me for newspapers, and I bought her *Cinema and Theatre* every week, the only illustrated magazine the Nazis had not been able to infect completely with their propaganda. Anne cut out the pictures of the actors she liked and pasted them on the wall. She knew she was not allowed to ask me for a newspaper, since her parents had forbidden her to see any, but she always looked so appealingly at me that I sometimes hid the newspaper in the inside pocket of my jacket for her, just for the pleasure of being able to look a little longer into those big, questioning eyes."

Miep says that she had heard about Anne's scribbling. She and her husband had previously known the child only slightly, from a few visits to the Franks; since Anne was in poor health at that time, she was sent promptly to bed after dinner. She used to obey grudgingly.

"Anne was a child, after all," Miep says, "and she was still that in the Secret Annexe. A small person, fourteen years old, who was in great trouble. But the adults up there were in trouble also, and when we came up they threw innumerable questions at us. What is it like outside? What is going on? We had to think and answer, and in answering consider quickly what we might tell them and what it would be better to conceal. Perhaps in the press of it we sometimes ignored Anne's quieter questions.

"But one day I went upstairs – it was in the afternoon and Anne was sitting alone at the table, writing. She was writing in an account book like those we had in the office. I recognised it. She promptly closed the book and put it away, blushing. At that moment Mrs Frank came into the room and said: 'Yes, we have a daughter who writes. Did you know that?' She said it in a tone that held pride – and at the same time loneliness and sadness that this child withdrew from her by writing. And I stood in front of them, looking at the child and her mother, and said: 'Really? I didn't know at all.'

"But I did know, of course."

Mr Koophuis also knew. He recalls a time during the noon hour when he had just had some sort of business vexation with Mr van Daan, and as he was about to go Mr van Daan asked whether he could not obtain cigarettes for him. Cigarettes were very hard to get at the time.

Anne had been sitting at the table, doing her homework. Suddenly she said:

"These people are already doing so much for us as it is. Do forget about the smoking, Mr van Daan. Otherwise Mr Koophuis will have to go trotting through half the town on your account."

The reproof hit home only too well, and van Daan left the room. Koophuis was about to leave, too. The incident had spoiled his temper. Suddenly Anne came to the door and said:

"Do you have a little time around four o'clock? Just a little."

Koophuis looked questioningly at her.

"I've put aside a cup of coffee for you. And I'd like to read a story to you."

Mr Koophuis came at four and Anne showed him her story, *Katrientje.*

"Of course we tried to keep in mind how hard it was for the child," Mr Koophuis says. "She was hungering for the world outside, for life with other children, and when my wife came up Anne would greet her with an almost unpleasant curiosity. She would ask about Corrie, our daughter. She wanted to know what Corrie was doing, what boy friends she had, what was happening at the hockey club, whether Corrie had fallen in love. And as she asked she would stand there, thin, in her washed-out clothes, her face snow-white, for they all had not been out of doors for so long. My wife would always bring something for her, a pair of sandals or a piece of cloth; but coupons were so scarce and we did not have enough money to buy on the black market. It would have been so nice if we could have brought her a letter from Corrie occasionally, but Corrie was not allowed to know that the Franks weren't abroad, as everyone thought, but were still in Amsterdam. We did not want to burden her with this almost unendurable secret.

"But then something happened.

"It was in November 1942, on Peter's birthday. We were all upstairs sitting over the birthday coffee, and we men were bent over a map of the theatres of war, discussing where the Allies would venture their first landing. I said in Spain, and Mr Frank said in Africa first. But Mr van Daan said: 'They will never land. They aren't coming…'

"Next morning I was still abed when I suddenly heard on the English radio that they had landed in Africa. And I called out to my wife, who was in the next room: 'There, you see, Mr Frank was right after all yesterday. They've landed in Africa.'

"Suddenly I saw my wife at the door. She gestured to me to be quiet, and pointed to Corrie's open door.

"A few days later, at the table Corrie was telling a story about school. She stumbled over and mispronounced a difficult name, and I corrected her. Suddenly she looked at me and said: 'You sometimes get names twisted, too, don't you?'

"After that she never said another word about it. But now she knew, and kept her silence. Children can be very loyal, to themselves and others, and Corrie was deeply attached to Anne."

*

What kind of people are these – Koophuis, Kraler, Elli, Miep and her husband? Simple people with great souls. They are reliable and matter-of-fact, and they do not talk much.

The Dutch are by nature loyal and close-mouthed, I have been told, and they can be incredibly obstinate. But Miep was not Dutch at all. She was born in Vienna. Kraler, too, is an Austrian by birth, and during the war Austria was part of Germany. They were just as much or as little German as Rauter, the Gestapo chief in the Netherlands, as the German Reich commissioner in The Hague, as Hitler, or as the police sergeant who later arrested the Franks. All of these people also came from Austria. The dark line is not a line around nations. It runs right through nations, through the German people also, although among us during those days the contrasting shade was dim and hidden.

Mr Kraler, then, is an Austrian. He fought in the Imperial Navy during World War I, and came to Holland afterward. In July 1933 he met Mr Frank in Amsterdam. Miep, too, was first sent to Holland after World War I as an 'undernourished child' in whom a welfare organisation had taken an interest.

She stayed in Amsterdam. In 1933 she met Mr Frank, who hired her to work for the Travis company. When Austria was absorbed by Germany, she was given a German passport. After the occupation of Holland in 1940 the newly founded 'German Girls' Club in the Netherlands' asked her to join. She told its envoys frankly why she did not care to. A few days later she was called to the German consulate. A stamp was placed in her passport limiting its validity to three months and she was informed that she had to become a Dutch citizen within three months or emigrate as a stateless person. Where she was to emigrate to, no one said. The German troops were everywhere in Europe.

There would have remained only the North Sea.

At this time Henk van Santen and Miep wanted to be married, but they needed documents that were obtainable only in Vienna. The least they could do was to send the passport as evidence of Miep's right to these papers. The passport, however, had the damning stamp. Mr Frank then advised them to have a photostat made of the first two pages of the passport – the stamp was on the third page. By means of this trick, and with the aid of an aged uncle in Vienna, the documents were assembled, and the two were able to marry in July 1941. By this time the passport had long since expired. The Dutch immigration authorities had hitherto helped out with a few rather dubious documents, but these did not suffice for the registrar's office. At the wedding Henk handed the passport across the desk to the registrar, at the same time giving him a sharp look. The registrar leafed through the pages of the passport, returned Henk's sharp look, then thrust the passport into his coat pocket and said: "The documents are in order."

But if Henk had not nudged Miep, she would have forgotten to say 'I do'.

I asked Miep and Henk about Anne's mother, about the van Daans, and about Düssel. Miep said:

"I saw Mrs Düssel sometimes. You see, she did not know where her husband was. She knew Anne, incidentally, and thought very highly of her."

Miep had felt intensely sorry for Mrs Düssel. Mr Düssel had been a cultivated and highly intelligent person, she said. Of course, life in the confined quarters of the Secret Annexe had made him rather difficult – but after all, what a difficult life that had been! Anne, she added, had described him in her diary with extreme severity.

Henk suddenly interrupted:

"I once read a story about two Australian flyers who made an emergency landing on the ice in the Antarctic. They lived for seven months in a cave in the ice. But the worst of it was, one of them wrote, not the ice and their fear and the solitude; the worst of it was that the other fellow made the same sound brushing his teeth every morning, and the same movement folding his trousers every night."

"Mr Düssel simply got on Anne's nerves," Miep went on. "That was chiefly it." Miep herself sometimes played the part of 'secret agent' with Mrs Düssel, and would bring her 'greetings' from her husband from abroad. At each of these times, Mrs Düssel rejoiced.

As for the van Daans, Miep describes Peter as a simple, lovable boy. Anne would sometimes tease him for his slow, methodical ways. But, she added, it was clear from the diary that she loved him, although she may rather have loved more her dream of love than the boy himself. That is, in a way her love passed by Peter, was a love directed towards the future…

"Mr van Daan was a highly intelligent and well-bred man. But in time his nervous strength gave out. Mrs van Daan, on the other hand, was a very uncomplicated person, anxious and cheerful at the same time, as temperamental people often are." But if anyone had a premonition of how badly it would all end, she was the one, Mrs van Daan. Perhaps Mrs Frank, too, although she was not at all anxious, rather humorous and kindly, often very quiet. The great love Margot always displayed towards her would be proof that Anne was also unjust in her description of her mother.

Abruptly, Miep added:

"Perhaps I ought not to talk about justice. In her own way she was just. You see, she was uncompromising. That's it. And we have all seen now that she was far less sparing of herself. How severely she judged herself… Still, she was the

106

happiest of all of them. For the others, those twenty-five months were nothing but misery. Margot, too, was sometimes terribly depressed. Only Anne felt that this period was also an adventure. She said so herself. You remember, she wrote: *I am young and strong and am living a great adventure.*"

Of them all, Elli was closest to Anne during this period. Elli is softhearted and defenceless, warm, candid, and shy at once. She was eight or nine years older than Anne, but in her heart Anne was not nearly so defenceless as she, and that lent Anne a certain advantage. Elli was engaged at the time, and had many problems, and since she had no one else to talk things over with, and Anne was right in the midst of her happy love affair with Peter, they became close friends. Elli says that often Anne seemed like a sister to her, and sometimes almost motherly, so superior did her happiness make her.

It was very odd, talking with Elli. She was a little uneasy and reserved at first, but after the initial awkwardness wore off there was scarcely any stopping her. Memories and images came pouring out of her, as fresh and new as when she had first apprehended them within herself thirteen and more years ago. There was nothing sifted out, nothing withheld. It was all as if it had happened yesterday, and all that separated her from yesterday was the loss of Anne.

It was only natural for Anne to be most closely attached to her father, Elli says. The two of them were alike. Mr Frank, too, she says, is a person with the kind of understanding one mostly finds only in writers. He, too, could be as affectionate as Anne, and he, too, was unsparing with himself.

When Elli read the diary, she remembered many little things that are not mentioned in the diary. For example, Anne once spoke to her about Moortje, her little tomcat, and said that she still longed for him, that she missed his loving ways. This feeling, she said, was sometimes stronger, sometimes weaker in her, but it was always present.

Another time, Anne read aloud to her something she had written: that Pim – this was what she called her father – was a great optimist, but he always found a reason for his optimism. Anne herself, Elli added, had never been an optimist, though certainly not a pessimist either. She was what she was.

Sometimes she was bad and nasty-tempered, Elli says. Then only her father could bring her to her senses, but he could do it with a single word. 'Self-control' was the magic formula, and he needed only to whisper it to her. It took immediate effect, for Anne was as keenly sensitive as her father, upon whom a soft word always made far more impression than any shouting.

Elli had the feeling that she could speak her mind to Anne. As I have said, she had troubles at this time, and she followed her instinct and found Anne a great support. She and Anne often sat together and chattered away, told each other stories and sometimes cried together.

Anne, though perfectly aware of the precariousness of their situation, had a great deal of confidence, a great trust in the future. Once, when she had again read a story to Elli, she suddenly asked:

"Could you manage to have them printed?"

Another time Elli asked Anne whether she really wanted to become a writer. Anne first replied yes, then no, then again yes, and finally she said with a sudden radiant smile: "No, I want to marry early and have many children!"

Oh, what plans we have all had!

*

Miep and Henk had told me that they had once spent a night in the Secret Annexe because the children so wanted to 'have guests'. But it had been a fearful and frightening night for the two of them, and only the others slept soundly, sheltered by their misery, guarded by their forlornness.

Now Elli told me that she, also, had spent a night in the hideout, sleeping on an air mattress. That was in October 1942, she said. She, too, had not closed an eye, had almost died of terror. Yet she had been lucky; there had been no air-raid alarm that night; all was quiet from dusk to dawn, and from all the rooms came only the sound of quiet breathing. But the building had creaked and crackled inside the walls and the old beams. Then there would be a gust of wind in the tree outside, and a car far away, coming closer and closer, sounding its horn once and coming steadily closer, until at last the tyres could be heard humming on the bridge over the canal – the awaited sign that the car had driven past. But then gears would suddenly crash somewhere out there in the darkness, sounds of grinding and clicking, and then the bell of the Westertoren would strike once and again – that was the half-hour – and in fifteen minutes it would strike again for the quarter of the hour, and when it struck again it would be two o'clock – how many quarter-hours are there in such a night?… The thing was not to wait for the striking, because if you waited the clock suddenly stopped striking and the quarter-hour became a hole growing ever blacker and bigger, and the car might come back, after all, and stop in front of the house, and then there would be the rap on the door – until you started up in bed, holding your head and saying: My God, it must be morning. And then, then the clock on the tower would strike, and it had been only a quarter-hour like all the other quarter-hours…

Elli had felt dead-beat next day. She had been unable to finish her work, and so she stayed late at the office, after all the others had gone. Suddenly the door opened and Anne's face appeared in the crack. She whispered:

"Has everyone left?"

Anne was in fine fettle, as she had been since the morning. She had slept perfectly well – she was accustomed to the grinding gears of night.

"Have they left, Elli?"

"Yes, long ago," Elli said.

Then Anne tiptoed across the big office, stooping so that no one could see her from the street. She posted herself behind the curtain and peered through a tiny opening in order to catch a glimpse, a prisoner's perspective, of the world.

During this period Anne acquired an odd view of the world. There are a few passages in one of her stories, *Blurry*, which she probably could not have written if she had been able to see more of the world than her oblique view of the chestnut tree and the sky, than the narrow, curtain-slit segment of street, canal, and the houses on the other quay.

Blurry

When Blurry was still quite small, a terrible idea came to him one day: to run away from Mother Bear and discover the great world. For days he was far less lively than usual because he was so occupied in thinking over his plans. One evening, on the fourth day, he finally figured it out. His plan was developed and needed only to be carried out. Early in the morning he would go out into the garden, being very quiet, of course, so that his owner, Miesje, would not notice. Then he would crawl through a hole under the hedge, and after that... yes, after that he would go ahead and discover the world!

This is what he did, and he did it all so quietly and skillfully that no one was aware of his escape until after he had been on his way for hours. His whole hide was smeared with earth and mud by the time he crawled out on the other side of the hedge, but a bear who wants to discover the world cannot let himself be held up by a little dirt. Eyes straight ahead so that he would not stumble over the stones,

Blurry padded out to the street, which could be reached by the narrow lane between the gardens. When he arrived in the middle of the street he was a little frightened by all the grownups, for he saw that he was not even noticed among their legs. I must keep nicely to the edge of the sidewalk, he thought, or else they'll knock me over. That was very sensible. You see, Blurry was very sensible. That is clear from his wanting to discover the world, small as he was.

So he trotted along keeping close to the edge of the sidewalk, and taking care not to be caught up in the crowd. But suddenly his little heart began beating like the blows of a hammer. Why was that? A big dark, black pit opened up right in front of him. It was a cellar hole. But Blurry did not know that, and he staggered. Did he have to go on down there? Anxiously, he looked around. But the trousered men's legs and the stockinged women's legs went right on quite normally, as if there were nothing to it, across the pit. Blurry had not yet recovered completely from his fright, and he followed them cautiously, step by step. And soon he was able to walk along the wall again.

Here I am going about in the great world, but where is the world itself? Blurry pondered. There are so many stockinged and trousered legs that I can't see the world at all. I think I am still too small to be able to discover the world. But that doesn't matter. When I am older I'll be bigger, too, and if I drink lots of milk with skin on it (at this thought all his hair stood on end) I'll be just as big as the human beings. Anyway, I'll walk on for a while longer. Somehow or other I'll manage to see something of the world.

Blurry went on, trying to be perturbed as little as possible by the fat and skinny legs around him. But did he really have to keep walking on and on? He was already terribly hungry, and besides it was beginning to grow dark in the street. Blurry had not counted on having to eat and sleep sooner or later. He had been far too busy with his explorer's plans to have thought of anything so ordinary and so unheroic as eating and sleeping. Sighing, he went on a little farther, until he came upon the open door of a house. Hesitantly, he paused, but then he made up his mind and cautiously went in. He was lucky, for after he had gone through a second doorway he saw two bowls standing between something with four wooden legs. One bowl had milk with skin on it, the other had solid food. Starving hungry and craving something good, Blurry drank the milk bowl dry in one gulp, and just like a grown-up bear did not let the skin on the milk bother him at all. After that he fell upon the food, until finally he felt filled and content.

But, O horrors, what was that coming? Something white with green eyes slowly approached, staring fixedly at him. It stopped right in front of him and asked in a high voice: "Who are you? And why have you eaten up my food?" "I am Blurry and I am out to discover the world. But food is necessary for that. That is why I have eaten this food. You see, I didn't know it was yours." "Aha, so you want to discover the world. But then why did you go and pick on my bowls?" "Because I did not see any others standing around," Blurry said with as much bluster as he could. But then he thought better of it, and asked in a somewhat more friendly way: "Who are you, anyway? And what kind of odd human being are you?" "I am Miura and I belong to the race of Angora cats. I am very valuable, my mistress always tells me. But you know what, Blurry, I'm often bored being so alone. Won't you stay with me for a while?" "I'll be glad to sleep here with you," Blurry replied cordially and with an expression that seemed to say he was doing beautiful Miura a special favor, "but tomorrow I must go on to discover the world." Miura indicated that she was content with that for the present.

"Come along," she said, and Blurry followed her into another room where again he saw nothing but legs. Fat wooden legs, big and small. But, oh yes, there was something else there. In a corner stood a big basket with a handsome green silk cushion. Without more ado Miura climbed up on this cushion, dirty paws and all. Blurry did not think it right to make everything so dirty. "Ought I not to wash up a bit first?" he asked. "I'll make you nice and clean the way I wash myself," Miura replied. Blurry had no idea what this method was, but that was just as well, for otherwise he would certainly not

have submitted to it. The cat ordered him around, told him to stand up straight. Then she calmly licked Blurry's paws clean with her tongue. Blurry shuddered and asked anxiously whether Miura always washed in this way? "Yes," she said, "you'll soon see how clean it makes you. You'll be spick-and-span, and a spick-and-span bear will be admitted to places much more easily and so will be far more successful at discovering the world."

Blurry did his best to repress his disgust. He clenched his teeth and like a brave bear did not let out a peep. But Miura's washing took a terribly long time. Blurry was beginning to grow awfully impatient. His feet hurt him from standing still so long. But at last, at last, he was spick-and-span. Miura climbed into the basket once more, and Blurry, who was now dead tired, lay down alongside. Within five minutes both of them were sound asleep.

Next morning Blurry woke up in a daze, and it was a while before he could recall where he was. Miura was still snoring a little, but Blurry wanted his breakfast. So without any consideration for his kind hostess, he shook her off him and at once began making demands: "How about breakfast, Miura? I'm frightfully hungry."

The beautiful Angora cat yawned, then stretched until she was twice her usual size. "There won't be anything more for you," Miura said. "My mistress must not find out that you are here. Slip out through the garden, and be quick about it."

She led him out of the room, through the door, then through another door, then through a third – this one was of glass. Then they were outside. Miura accompanied him as far as the gate. "Have a good trip, Blurry, and good-by," she said, and was gone.

Feeling lonely and no longer so sure of himself, Blurry tramped across the garden, crawled through a hole under the hedge, and emerged on the street. Where should he go now? And how much longer would it take before he discovered the world? Blurry did not know. Slowly he walked along, until suddenly a big four-legged thing came around the corner at top speed. It made such a thunderous noise that Blurry's ears rang. Frightened, he pressed as close as he could against the stone wall of a house. The monster stopped near him, and then came close up to him. Blurry began to cry, but the big thing paid no attention to that. On the contrary, it sat down and looked wide-eyed at the poor little bear. Blurry trembled hard, but then he plucked up his courage and asked, "What do you want of me?" "I only want to look at you, for I have never seen anything like you."

Blurry breathed easier. So it was possible to converse with this huge thing. That was odd – back home he used to try and converse with his mistress, but she had never understood him. However, he did not have much time to think over this important question, for the big animal opened its mouth so wide that Blurry could see all its teeth. At this he was even more horrified than he had been by Miura's washing. What would the big thing do with him now? Well, he found out sooner than he liked, for without a by-your-leave the animal seized him by the back of the neck and carried him across the street. Blurry could not cry, for that would have choked him. He could not scream either. There was nothing for him to do but tremble, although that did not help to give him any fresh courage. Still, he did not have to walk, and if only his neck had not hurt so much, it would not have been so bad. But the rocking motion was making him dizzy, and where were they going? Where… Blurry fell asleep while the animal was still holding him tightly. But his slumber did not last long, for the big animal suddenly forgot why it had taken the little fellow along. Casually, it let Blurry drop, after biting him hard in the back of the neck, and ran off.

So there the helpless little bear lay, alone with his pain. But then he got to his feet, for he did not want to be run over. He rubbed his eyes and looked around. There were far less legs, far fewer human beings, far fewer stones underfoot, and there was much more sun here. Could this be the world at last?…

He heard noise behind him and turned around in alarm. Was another animal coming to bite him? But no, it was a little girl who had seen Blurry. "Look at that, Mummy, a little bear? Can I take him with me?" she asked her mother. "Oh, no, child, it's a sick bear.

114

See, it's bleeding." "It's just one cut. We can wash it off at home. I'll take him, and from now on I'll have something to play with."

Of course Blurry did not understand what they were saying, for little bears understand only the language of animals; but the little blonde-haired girl looked so sweet that he made no resistance when he was wrapped in a cloth and placed in the shopping bag. And so Blurry continued his journey into the world, swaying back and forth.

After a while the little girl took him into her arms. That was a piece of good fortune, for now he could see the world from higher up for the first time. What a huge heap of stones lay before him, and how they were all piled one on top of the other. How high they were, with here and there a white hole between them, and right at the top, almost in heaven, surely intended as an ornament like the feather on his owner's hat, a little smoke came out... That was jolly. Above the stones there seemed to be something else that was all blue. But look, something moved, covered the blue, and came closer and closer to him, until it hung right over his head, and after that it was as blue up there as before, and down on the street something honked and ran very fast, but where were the paws or legs it was running on? There were none. It certainly was worthwhile discovering the world...

At last, at last, the girl stopped in front of a door. They went in, and the first thing Blurry caught sight of was something like Miura. This sort of creature was called a cat; he remembered that very well now. This cat rubbed against the blonde girl's legs, but she chased it away and carrying Blurry went up to something white. It was high above the floor, wide, white and smooth. The girl began washing Blurry, especially at the spot on his hide where the queer animal had bitten him. That was very painful, and Blurry cried hard, but no one paid any attention to his crying. Fortunately the washing did not last long, and then he was dried. The girl tied a clean band of cloth around his neck and put him into a bed like the one he had had at his mistress's home. But why should he be in bed now? He was not a bit tired. And no sooner had the girl gone out the door than he jumped out of the bed and ran through many doors to the street.

115

Now I really must have something to eat, Blurry thought. He sniffed the air – somewhere in the vicinity there must be food, for he could smell it. He followed his nose, and soon he was standing at the door from which the odor came. Slipping between the legs of a woman, he found himself in a big store. Behind the counter stood two girls, who quickly noticed him. They had a great deal to do and could probably use his assistance. Immediately they seized him and placed him in a dark room where it was terribly hot. But that was not so bad, since here he could eat as much as he wanted. On the floor and on low benches round about lay rows and rows of rolls and cakes; never in his life had he seen so many or such wonderful things to eat. He fell upon the goodies and began eating like mad, and soon he had eaten so much that he felt almost sick. Then he took the time to look around him. It was a real paradise here… Nothing but white legs, very different from the way it was out in the street. But he was not allowed much time for dreaming. The girls had been watching him, and now they thrust a big broom into his hand and showed him how to use it. He set bravely to work, but it was not so simple as it looked. The broom was heavy, and the dust tickled his nostrils. He had to sneeze constantly. Whenever ever he wanted to rest, someone would come at once and order him to keep working, and even give him a slap. I might really have done without this, Blurry thought. But now there was no help for it. He had to sweep, and so he swept. After he had been sweeping for a long time, long enough to sweep all the dirt into a huge heap, one of the girls led him to a corner where there was a pile of loose, yellow, hard curly stuff. She laid him down, and Blurry understood that he would now be allowed to sleep. He stretched out comfortably, and slept and slept as though the pile of excelsior were the finest bed in the world.

He had to get up at seven. Once more he was allowed to eat as many bakestuffs as he wished, but afterward he had to go back to work. Poor Blurry! Besides, he really had not even had enough sleep… For the first time he began to long for home… How would he ever manage to get back there? Blurry had to wait, wait and hope, and he suddenly felt weak and confused. Everything began to whirl around him, so that he had to sit down… But one grows accustomed to anything, and after a week Blurry no longer knew that he had ever done anything but sweep. Little bears forget fairly fast. And that was fortunate. But still he had not forgotten his mother and his former home. Only they now seemed unreal and unattainably far away.

One evening the two girls in the shop read the following advertisement in the newspaper: "Reward for the honest finder of a small brown bear who answers to the name of Blurry…"

"Could this be our bear?" they asked themselves. "He doesn't do very much anyhow. It might be more profitable to collect the reward. Let us take him back." They quickly ran into the bakery and called: "Blurry!"

Blurry came. "You see, that is his name!" the girls said. "We'll take him back right away, this evening."

That was nice. The same evening Blurry was brought to his mistress, and the girls received their reward.

From his mistress Blurry received a good spanking for his naughtiness, and then a kiss because he was back. But from his mother he received only the following greeting:

"Blurry, why did you run away?"

"I wanted to discover the world," Blurry answered.

"And did you discover it?"

"Oh, I saw a lot, a great deal, and now I am a very clever bear."

"I know that. But I asked whether you discovered the world."

"No… not really. I could not find the world!"

CHAPTER 8

More Deadlines

In 1941 Seyss-Inquardt, Reich Commissioner for the Occupied Netherlands, licensed the *Jüdische Wochenblatt* in Amsterdam. This newspaper was intended by the German authorities to keep the Jewish community abreast of police orders. Its first issues read like a club newspaper. They are made up of general observations and news items, announcements of social, professional, and religious events, and strive in a somewhat forced manner for an innocuous, unalarmed tone. In the course of the next several years, however, the newspaper grew thinner and more taciturn. Decrees of the occupying Power take up more space, general news items vanish, comment is restricted to religious subjects. Crude, poor newsprint is used. The text affects one like a thin, spectral hymn sung above a yawning pit. Editorial observations are terse and fervent as prayers.

The issue of September 25th, 1943, contained an editorial on the coming New Year celebration. It contained such phrases as these:

'In the Jewish conception of the world... New Year's Day is a day of recollection... We expect that each man will conscientiously examine his life and his acts. But above all it is a day for recollecting God. It is the day... on which all generations pass before His eye, on which deeds are weighed and fates decided. Fearfully, mankind encounters the Godhead... for now the lot of man and the destiny of the cosmos are regarded from Eternity and indissolubly linked with Eternity. Now men's fates come before the day of judgment, and God passes the sentence of history...'

The most terrible year in the suffering-laden history of this ancient people was done. The year 5704 of the Jewish calendar began. No one in Amsterdam will ever forget this New Year's celebration, for this New Year proved worse than the old one had been.

Some time before, a particular phrase had become established as slogan and code word among the German authorities inside the Reich and in the occupied territories. The phrase for the elimination of the European Jews was: 'Final solution of the Jewish question'. Behind this gruesome, ostensibly harmless but slyly transparent bit of officialese were concealed fantastic ideas, and ultimately acts for which no descriptive adjective suffices. One of the earliest official inspirations was the insane project of settling the Jews in a Jewish state in Madagascar. Dr Hjalmar Schacht, the realist, opposed this and urged general emigration of the Jews to countries of their own choosing; he also hoped that foreign countries would ransom the Jews' confiscated property by extending a loan of several billions to Germany.

The events of the war nullified both the romantic and the businesslike plans, and after the victories in Poland and the Ukraine more concrete ideas were discussed. Reinhard Heydrich, Chief of the Sicherheitsdienst (Security Police), made a proposal at a meeting held on January 20th, 1942 in Berlin:

"In squadrons, with the sexes separated, Jews fit for work will be taken to these areas, in the course of which a large part of them will undoubtedly be eliminated by natural decease. The residue eventually remaining at the end, since it will undoubtedly be the most resistant portion, will have to be treated as required since, representing a natural selection, it would have to be regarded in case of release as the germinal cell of a new Jewish upsurge."[4]

Five important members of the SD and ten civilian representatives from various ministries took part in this conference. The minutes of the session were circulated through all the top offices of the Government. Copy 16 played a part in later war-criminal trials.

The actual outcome of all the plans was the system of annihilation camps. From 1942 on, Auschwitz was going full blast. In this realm, too, officialese fulfilled its function. For cattle truck deliveries of living human beings it devised the term 'transplacement', and for mass murder the expression 'special treatment'.

Dr H H Kremer, a former professor of the University of Münster and an SS officer with the rank of captain, noted in his Auschwitz diary:

'2/9/42 – Present for the first time at a "special action" at three o'clock in the morning. In comparison to this, Dante's inferno seems to me a comedy…

'5/9/42 – This afternoon present at a special action from the women's KZ [concentration camp]… Dr Thilo is right in what he said to me today, that here we are in the *anus mundi*. Toward 8.00pm at another special action from Holland…

'6–7/9/42 – Today we had an excellent lunch: tomato soup, half a chicken with potatoes and red cabbage, pudding and excellent vanilla ice cream… Outside again at 8.00pm for a special action.

'9/9/42 – Took part in a special action in the evening (four times). How many doubles do I have in this world?'

The doctor's question is difficult to answer. Certainly, he was not alone; there is ample evidence for that. Rauter,

---

[4] In translating this, as well as other Nazi documents in this book, we have taken pains to reproduce as literally as possible the peculiar abstractness of the deadly gibberish employed by Nazi spokesmen – The translators.

Gestapo chief of the Netherlands, had written to Himmler in the letter quoted earlier:

'On October 15th the Jews in Holland will be declared outlaws; that is, a large-scale police operation will be set in motion. Not only the German and Dutch police will be enlisted for this, but also the labour groups of the National Socialist Party, the Party branches, the NSB [the Dutch Nazi party], the Army, etc. Every Jew found anywhere in Holland...'

In reality this 'action' began somewhat earlier. The 22,000 relatives of the 8,000 Jews assembled in the labour camps had, contrary to Rauter's expectations, by no means all responded obediently to the decrees published on October 1st. They had to be rounded up. This was done mainly at night, when the Jews were required to remain in their homes. There they sat together, knapsacks already packed. The children were sleeping. They waited for the ring of the doorbell. The streets resounded with the tramp of boots, the thunder of trucks, and screams.

Rauter had also written:

'Simultaneously I am issuing proclamations declaring that Aryans who have kept Jews hidden, smuggled Jews across the border, or falsified identity papers, will have their property confiscated and will themselves be sent to a concentration camp.'

He did not mention his more confidential methods of work. No doubt he could assume that Heinrich Himmler was familiar with them. In the Rijksinstituut voor Oorlogsdocumentatie (National Institute for Documents of the War) in Amsterdam is a collection of receipts for seven gulden and fifty cents which the police paid out for each arrested Jew, and official forms for rewarding the denouncers of 'Jews in flight'; there was a space on these forms where the amount of the reward was to be entered in ink. In an address to the Netherlands SS Rauter said:

"It is my endeavour to dispose of the Jews as quickly as possible. This is not a pretty assignment, but it is a great work. The Germanic SS will show no pity if the whole Germanic race stands behind it. Whoever does not understand this and speaks of pity and humanism cannot be a leader in these times."

Rauter carried out his 'assignment', and when his teams had become sufficiently practised in the forcible removal of people by innumerable individual 'actions', he issued orders for the grand onslaught. On October 2nd, 1942, 14,000 Jews were deported from Holland, on May 26th, 1943, 3,000, and on June 20th, 5,700 were arrested in Amsterdam alone. The 'transplacement' of the Jews was in full swing.

In the archives of the Rijksinstituut there are many photographs of these 'actions', most of them taken from the files of the German propaganda department. The photographs show Jews in the streets, singly, in families, in whole 'herds'. We see them at the assembly points, some with heads held high, some with heads bowed, astonished, despairing, faces full of contempt and faces utterly shattered. And the others may be seen, too, in their high boots, armed with carbines and submachine guns. Among them there always stands one checking off a list. Numbering went on, a kind of satyr play upon the wreckage of justice.

In these pictures I saw virtually all the uniforms worn by German men in the services – not only the tunics of the SS. Men from other services can be seen among the active participants, and among the spectators.

The issue of the *Judische Wochenblatt* whose editorial I have quoted was, incidentally, the last issue of this newspaper. Four days after its publication, on the eve of the New Year, ten thousand Amsterdam Jews were flushed from their houses and deported. The editors of the newspaper were included, since no more official proclamations were needed now.

These things were done in our times, in our midst. There were such meetings, such minutes and initials on documents, such diary entries, such letters, newspaper articles, and acts.

I asked Koophuis, Elli, Miep, and Henk how much of this the eight fugitives in the Secret Annexe had known. Elli said:

"They knew everything. At least they suspected everything. It is all there in Anne's diary. Anne herself once saw two Jews passing by in the street, when she was in the office with me, peeping through the crack in the curtain. And there was not a Jew walking in the street whose look did not tell the whole story."

Koophuis says:

"When we had our plate of soup upstairs with them at noon, we tried to say nothing about what was happening outside. But it could not be concealed. The air was charged with it. It penetrated through the walls. Almost everything happened at night, you know, when we, too, were back at home. But we all heard the roar of the cars, the stopping, the pounding on the doors, heard it even in our beds. We could even hear the frightful ring of the bell, so exactly did we know what was happening. There were nights when you had the feeling that in all Amsterdam bells were ringing and fists pounding on doors. And they, too, lived through those nights."

Miep says:

"We were no longer keeping silence; we had lost the habit of speech. Do you understand the difference? My husband and I sublet our place from a Jewish landlady. She had a married daughter and two grandchildren, three and five years old. One day her daughter and son-in-law were picked up in a street raid, with these two children. Our landlady hid in someone's else's flat that night, since we expected that they would also comb through the houses. In the middle of the night the doorbell rang suddenly, and when we opened the door, there was a girl in the hallway, with the two children. She said that first the SS had taken them all along, but all at once, in a dark street, one of the auxiliary policemen had come up to her, thrust the two children at her, and told her to take them home.

"Our landlady came back the next day. When she saw the children, she abandoned the flat and found a hiding place somewhere with them.

"We had said nothing all the while that we saw only inhumanity. But now that we perceived that in the midst of all this bestiality a spark was sometimes possible, a spark of humanity – it amounted to nothing, of course, since the same policeman had taken the two parents along, but still it was a spark, an incomprehensible spark – when we saw that, we did not dare even to think any longer."

These things were done, in our times. But there was also resistance.

Henk, who is a social worker on a Dutch welfare board, says:

"My associates and I were on field work. People from our office would visit the sick and old and help them out. One noon I came back to the office and went to wash my hands. One of my colleagues came up to the washbowl beside me and said softly: 'Henk, we need another few men.'

"I nodded."

Thereafter, whenever Henk went out on field work, someone would pass him a slip of paper containing a list of addresses of persons in hiding. Not only Jews were living underground. The Gestapo were also looking for political opponents, and many others were hiding because they had been called up for forced labour in Germany. The organisation Henk now belonged to supplied these people, in their attics, cellars, and other hide-outs, with money and ration cards. The fugitives knew the watchword, and until it was given they would not expose themselves to their stealthy visitors. But these precautions did not offer complete protection. The police often attempted to trap the resistance members.

Henk relates:

"We had keys to the houses and apartments, for if we had rung the bell, no one would ever have opened the door. But I always listened before I entered, and twice I heard German being spoken inside. In those cases I cleared out quickly."

Koophuis guessed what Henk was doing. Miep found out after a few weeks had passed. She says:

"I did not try to stop my husband. I was terrified for him, for I do love him. If I had not loved him, perhaps I could not have endured wondering in terror every single day: Will he come home today?"

CHAPTER 9

The Final Solution

Henk says: "On August 4th I was again going my rounds. As it approached noon I went to the Prinsengracht to eat with Miep and the others. We always had lunch together, you see.

"I went to the building and up the stairs, but as I opened the office door Miep rushed up to me and whispered sharply: 'Gestapo!'

"Just that one word. And as she said it she pressed her purse with our money and ration cards into my hand, and I gave her the bread I had brought and left quickly. There was no one in the street, nor had I seen anyone in the building. I reached my office safely. It was only seven minutes from the Prinsengracht, but I was glad when I arrived there. I took out everything I had in my pockets, the list with the addresses of the strangers I was supposed to visit that day, put it all into my desk drawer, and locked the drawer. Then I considered for a moment, and then I went back to the Prinsengracht."

What happened in the house on the Prinsengracht on that fourth of August, 1944, was far less dramatic than it is now depicted on the stage. In reality the cars did not approach with howling sirens, did not stop with screaming brakes in front of the house. The bell was not rung. No rifle butt rapped against the door till it reverberated as it now reverberates in the theatre every night somewhere in the world. The truth was, at first no one heard a sound. *They* were practised, skilful, and quiet in such cases.

Mr Koophuis says:

"It was a Friday, and a fine August day. The sun was

shining; we were working in the big office, Miep, Elli, and myself, and in the warehouse below us the spice mills were rumbling.

"When the sun was shining the trees along the canal and the water itself would often cast flecks of light on the ceiling and walls of the office, ripples of light that flickered and danced. It was an odd effect, but we knew then that it was fair outside."

Mr Frank says:

"It was about half past ten. I was upstairs in the van Daan's part of the house, in Peter's room, doing schoolwork with him. Nothing could be heard. And if there really was anything to hear, I was at any rate not paying attention. I had just been giving Peter English dictation, and was saying to him: 'Why, Peter, you know that *double* is spelled with only one *b* in English.'"

Elli says:

"Mr Koophuis and Miep were writing and I was posting entries in the receipts book when a car drove up in front of the house. But cars often stopped, after all. Then the front door opened, and someone came up the stairs. I wondered who it could be. We often had callers. Only this time I could hear that there were several men…"

Miep says:

"The footsteps moved along the corridor; then a door creaked, and a moment later the connecting door to Mr Kraler's office opened, and a fat man thrust his head in and said in Dutch: 'Quiet. Stay in your seats.'

"I started, and at first did not know… but then I knew."

Mr Koophuis continues:

"I suppose I did not hear them because of the rumbling

of the mills downstairs. The fat man's head was the first thing I saw, and then the door opened a little farther and I saw that there was another man standing in front of Kraler, asking him something. I think Kraler answered him. He was sitting at his desk, saying something, and then he rose slowly to his feet and went out with the man. I heard them on the stairs. There was nothing more he could do now.

"The fat man came in and planted himself in front of us. 'You three stay here, understand?' he barked.

"So we stayed in the office and listened as someone else went upstairs, and doors rattled, and then there were footsteps everywhere. They searched the whole building."

Mr Kraler wrote this account:

"It was a very fine summer day. Suddenly a staff sergeant of the 'Green Police' and three Dutch civilians entered my office and asked me for the owner of the house. I gave them the name and address of our landlord. No, they said to me, we want the person who is in charge here. That is myself, I replied. Then, 'Come along,' they ordered.

"The police wanted to see the storerooms in the front part of the building, and I opened the doors for them. All will be well if they don't want to see anything else, I thought. But after the sergeant had looked at everything, he went out into the corridor, ordering me again to come along. At the end of the corridor they drew their revolvers all at once and the sergeant ordered me to push aside the bookcase at the head of the corridor and open the door behind it. I said: 'But there's only a bookcase there!' At that he turned nasty, for he knew everything. He took hold of the bookcase and pulled at it; it yielded and the secret door was exposed. Perhaps the hooks had not been properly fastened. They opened the door, and I had to precede them up the steps. The policemen followed me; I could feel their pistols in my back. But since the steps were only wide enough for a single person, I was the first to enter the Franks' room. Mrs Frank was standing at the table. I made a great effort and managed to say: 'The Gestapo is here.'

"She did not start in fright, nor say anything in response."

Otto Frank continues:

"I was pointing out to Peter his mistakes in the dictation when someone suddenly came running up the stairs. The steps creaked, and I started to my feet, for it was morning when everyone had to be quiet – but then the door flew open and a man stood before us holding his pistol aimed at my chest. The man wore civilian clothes.

"Peter and I raised our hands. The man told us to step forward, and we had to walk past him, and then he ordered us to go downstairs, while he followed us with the pistol.

"Downstairs all the others were already assembled. My wife and the children and the van Daans were standing there with raised hands. Then Düssel came in, followed by another stranger. In the middle of the room stood a 'Green policeman'. He scrutinised our faces."

Miep later found out the name of this 'Green policeman'. We will call him S.

The witnesses all agree that he was a stocky man of medium height, middle-aged, and that his face was not unpleasant, not icy or cruel, at any rate. Miep says:

"He looked as though he might come round tomorrow to read your gas meter or punch your tram ticket."

The 'Green policeman' was accompanied by four or five Dutch Nazis. They wore plain-clothes and were 'eager beavers', behaving rather like the detectives in a movie thriller.

After the war Mr Koophuis identified these men from an album of photographs shown to him by a war-crimes investigating commission. One of them, he said, was about fifty-five, the fat man about forty-five, the others somewhat younger. He told me that the Gestapo employed a great many such civilian agents. For the most part, they were men who were failures in life; there were criminals among them. But there were also some who had swallowed the Nazi line, and believed that what they were doing was good and right.

None of the occupants of the Secret Annexe had seriously counted on the possibility that they would be discovered. The terrors they had suffered at the beginning, the terrors of those first nights, which each had had to bear by himself, were by now largely faded. Only Mr van Daan had continued to have occasional fits of despair; he had once hinted to Mr Frank that he could no longer endure life and that he would prefer the whole thing to be over, one way or another – he did not say precisely what he meant by this last phrase. But these crises were not due to premonitions of evil. He was worn out, while the others, the womenfolk, too, had become accustomed to the life they were leading.

In recent weeks, however, even Mr van Daan had been in good spirits. The war was clearly approaching an end. Every news report made that clear, even the German Army communiqués. The Russians were well into Poland; in Italy the Allies had reached Florence. American forces had broken through at Avranches, and the armies landed in Normandy were pouring with tremendous power into the heart of France. At the moment a solid German western front no longer existed, and it looked as though no new one would be formed until Holland was liberated. Twenty-five months had passed since Anne had made her diary entry describing their arrival at the house on the Prinsengracht. Fear cannot be maintained for twenty-five months. They were now full of confidence. Only two months before, Anne had written:

> *Perhaps, Margot says, I may yet be able to go back to school in*
> *September or October.*

And although such incidents as the burglary in April could still throw them into a fever of nervousness, their confidence had returned so quickly that Anne was able to describe the scene in almost comic terms:

> *I prepared myself for the return of the police, then we'd have to say that we were in hiding; they would either be good Dutch people, then we'd be saved, or N.S.B.-ers [Dutch Nazis], then we'd have to bribe them!*
>   *'In that case destroy the radio,' sighed Mrs van Daan. 'Yes, in the stove!' replied her husband. 'If they find us, then let them find the radio as well!'*
>   *'Then they will find Anne's diary,' added Daddy. 'Burn it then,' suggested the most terrified member of the party... 'Not my diary; if my diary goes, I go with it!' But luckily Daddy didn't answer.*

"And now they stood before us," Mr Frank says. "No, I had not imagined for so much as a moment what it would be like when they came. It was simply unthinkable. And now there they were.

"'Where is the storeroom?' they had asked downstairs. And now they asked: 'Where are your valuables?'

"I pointed to the cupboard where my cashbox was kept. The 'Green policeman' took it out. Then he looked around and reached for Anne's briefcase. He shook everything out, dumped the contents on the floor, so that Anne's papers and notebooks and loose sheets lay scattered all over the floorboards. Then he put our valuables into the briefcase, closed it, and asked us whether we had any weapons. But we had none, of course; anyway the plain-clothes men had already searched us thoroughly.

"Then he said: 'Get ready. All of you be back here in five minutes.'

"The van Daans went upstairs to fetch their knapsacks; Anne and Düssel went into their room, adjoining ours, and I reached for my knapsack, which hung on the wall. Suddenly the Gestapo man stopped in front of my wife's bed, stared down at the chest that stood between bed and window, and exclaimed: 'Where did you get this chest?'

"It was a grey foot-locker bound in iron, the kind we all had in the First War, and on the lid the words: 'Reserve Lieutenant Otto Frank.'

" 'It is my own,' I said.

" 'How did you get it?'

" 'I was an officer in the First War.'

"The man became exceedingly confused. He stared at me, and finally said:

" 'Then why didn't you report your status?'

"I bit my lips.

" 'Why, man, you would have been treated decently! You would have been sent to Theresienstadt.'

"I said nothing. Apparently he thought Theresienstadt a rest camp, so I said nothing. I merely looked at him. But he suddenly evaded my eyes, and all at once the perception came to me: Now he is standing at attention. Inwardly, this police sergeant had snapped to attention; if he dared, he might very well raise his hand to his cap in salute.

"Then he abruptly turned on his heel and raced upstairs. A moment later he came running down, and then he ran up again, and so he went, up and down, up and down, calling out: 'Take your time!'

"He shouted these same words to us and to his agents."

Mr Kraler writes:

"They were all utterly calm. They did not wail and lament. There was not much time for lamentations, for they had to pack their things, and so none of them betrayed their real feelings.

"It was now about noon, and I asked the sergeant whether I could bring my sandwiches up from the office. He said I might, so I went downstairs and fetched my lunch. Elli was crying terribly, and Mr Koophuis was sitting at his desk, staring into space. Then I went down to the storerooms, went very fast. The door stood open, and I was on the point of going out into the street, but then I saw another policeman. So I went back upstairs and ate my lunch in Mr Frank's old private office, while one man stood in front of me with a pistol in his hand."

Koophuis says:

"It all took a long time. The fat man had left the office, and we three were alone again. But we could not make an escape. The house is guarded, we thought. I considered: What was the first thing I had to do? And the next? And the thought kept running in my head: If only we hadn't involved the two girls.

"I said to Miep: 'Try and get away. They may let you through. Go to my house and see whether you can help my wife and Corrie. They will certainly search my home.'

"But Miep said she could not go now, that Henk had not come yet and now it was noon and he was sure to be along any moment. Then I tried the telephone. It was still working. I called my brother and told him what had happened, and he said at once: 'I'll go over to your house.'

"I hung up. Elli was standing at the window, crying and wringing her hands. You know, she was twenty-three, but at that moment she was nothing but a child. I left my desk, went over to her and said: 'Here, take my briefcase to the chemist on the corner. Tell him my brother will come and pick it up.'

"She took the briefcase at once, and left, and I thought: If they let her through, at least one of us is saved."

Elli, small defenceless Elli, relives her terror as she relates:

"I can't, can't describe it to you – it was so horrible. I prayed and prayed, and cried, and fell on my knees, and wished for only one thing: Let it be over quickly.

"I took the briefcase from Mr Koophuis and left. But at the front door, downstairs, my legs suddenly would not obey me. I thought: Suppose one of them is standing outside the door now. But I couldn't go back up to the office either, not for anything, and so I took the plunge and went out into the street. The street was deserted, no car, nothing to stop me. Henk was just coming down the street, but I didn't stop, I just ran away."

Koophuis says:

"After Henk had left, I said to Miep: 'Now you can go, too, Miep.' I pleaded with her to go, because there was no doubt about what they were going to do to us. But she would not leave."

Miep says:

"I couldn't leave. I think that was it: I simply couldn't go."

Koophuis:

" 'You must know what you're about,' I said to Miep. 'At least take the office keys. Here they are. And do your best to steer clear of it. *You* can't save us. Save what still can be saved. Just deny everything, do you hear? First and foremost make sure you are not involved.' "

Miep:

"Mr Koophuis gave me the keys to the office and I put them into my desk, but I just could not leave."

Elli says:

"Luckily the chemist was in. He took me to his back room, but I said nothing to him about the Franks. I only said we had had a radio in the office, and that they had caught us. Radio sets had been banned for some time. The chemist believed my story. He took the briefcase from me and promised to give it to Mr Koophuis's brother when he came. Then I asked whether I could use his telephone, and I called the office. Mr Koophuis answered. I asked him what I should do now, but I could hardly talk. Mr Koophuis considered for just a moment; then he said that I ought to go home. But as I started crying again, he suggested: 'Elli, if you want to, you can come back here. Perhaps one cannot escape fate…'

"But I cried out: 'No, no, I can't, I can't, I can't…'

"So I hung up and stayed there, sitting with the chemist and crying and praying. I stayed a long time, longer than an hour, maybe."

Miep says:

"They must certainly have been in the building for at least an hour when one of the plain-clothes men came down, took a chair, and sat down in front of me, at my desk. He called some office and ordered a car to be sent over. 'But a big one!' he added. 'There are seven or eight of them.' The voice on the telephone answered something, and the man said Yes and Good. Then he left us alone again."

Mr Frank says:

"They gave us more time than we needed. We all knew

what we had to pack – the same belongings we had planned on taking in case of fire.

"Once Anne came to me and I said 'No, don't take that, but you can take that along.' And she obeyed, for she was very quiet and composed, only just as dispirited as all the rest of us. Perhaps that was why she did not think to take along one of her notebooks, which lay scattered about on the floor. But perhaps, too, she had a premonition that all was lost now, everything, and so she walked back and forth and did not even glance at her diary.

"No one wept. It was just that all of us were terribly dispirited. None of us said a word more than was absolutely necessary. In any case these policemen had distributed themselves among the rooms and watched us while we packed. The Gestapo man could still be heard on the steps. And at last the van Daans came down. We were ready by then, too, and so we went out one after the other, through the open door. We left our hiding place, and went along the corridor and down the stairs. In the private office we had to wait again. Mr Kraler was already there when we came in, and now Mr Koophuis entered, and one of the agents took up a position between the two of them. The 'Green policeman' wanted to interrogate them, but both of them stated they had nothing to say to him. At that he exclaimed: 'All right, then you'll come along too.'"

Miep:

"And I heard them going, first in the corridor and then down the stairs; I could hear the heavy boots and the light footsteps, and then the very light footsteps of Anne. Through the years she had taught herself to walk so softly that you could hear her only if you knew what to listen for.

"I had seen her only the day before, and I was never to see her again, for the office door was closed as they all passed by."

Henk says:

"From my office I went back to the Prinsengracht, but I stayed on the other side of the canal, posted myself on the quay and looked across the water. After a while Mr Koophuis's brother came and joined me. But we could not see what was going on inside the building, for while I had been away a big closed police van had driven up, and was parked so close to the door that we could not see who was coming out and going in."

Mr Frank:

"Our two warehouse clerks stood in the front entrance as we came down, M and the other one, but I did not look as I passed them, and in memory I can only see their faces as pale, blank discs which did not move."

Koophuis:

"I was the first to step out into the street. People were standing around on the pavement, staring as if there had been a traffic accident. They all looked stunned.

"I was also the first to get into the van, and sat down in front, behind the driver. Suddenly I saw a man sitting opposite me, but in the darkness I could not make out his face. As the others were getting into the van and finding places on the bench, the driver glanced at me for just a moment through his window and whispered to me: 'Be careful. Don't talk now. He's one, too.' And he gave a slight nod of his head at the man in the corner. I nearly said something, but just then the bell of the Westertoren struck overhead."

Miep:

"I cannot say how late it was by now. I did not count the strokes of the bell, but it must have been noon. I stood behind the curtain, looking down at the street. The van had driven so close to the building that I had only a glimpse of the van Daans. They were deathly pale, but quite calm."

Henk says:

"From across the canal we heard the driver starting the motor, and then the van drove slowly down along the Prinsengracht as far as the Leliegracht, crossed the Lelie bridge, turned down the street and passed close by us. It went as far as the corner, then continued in the direction of Euterpe Straat, where the Gestapo headquarters was located. It is only a five-minute drive."

Miep says:

"Now I was alone in the building. I do not know whether the warehouse clerks were still downstairs in the storeroom. But I was alone upstairs, and after they drove off I sat down at my desk again and thought: Oh God…

"After a while I heard footsteps on the stairs, and S. and one of the Dutch civilians came in. The civilian said:

"'Her? She was in on it, too. Sure.'

"I denied it.

"Then S. sent the Dutchman out, and he planted himself in front of me and said: 'And what am I going to do with you?'

"He spoke in German, and I said: 'You're from Vienna, aren't you?'

"He was startled, so I said: 'I can tell from your speech. I am from Vienna, too.'

"When he asked for proof, I showed him my identity card. There it stood. He tossed the identity card on to the desk and exclaimed: 'And weren't you ashamed to help that Jewish trash?'

"I thought of what Mr Koophuis had said, and replied: 'I knew nothing about it.'

"But he said: 'You did!' He insisted on it, and we argued back and forth, until I began to see that he didn't know what he ought to do with me. He picked up the identity card again, read it through once more, and then he slapped it violently down on the desk for the second time and said: 'I tell you what, I'm going to let you go. But just as a personal favour and for no other reason, do you hear? And you stay right here. You come to the office every day, as usual; then at least I'll know what you're doing. If you disappear we'll take your husband just like that, understand?'

" 'My husband hasn't anything to do with the whole affair!'

" 'Don't give me any of that. He knows perfectly well what has been going on.'

"He turned on his heel and left, slamming the door behind him so hard that the frosted glass rattled, and then he ran down the stairs. I went to the window and saw him coming out of the house with a bicycle. He wheeled it along for a short distance, because the Prinsengracht is a one-way street, but at the corner he mounted it and rode off."

Elli adds:

"All afternoon I wandered through the city, not knowing where I was going, and did not reach home until dusk. My father was in bed. He had been operated on, some time before. But when the doctors saw that he had cancer of the stomach, they could do nothing for him.

"I sat down beside his bed and told him everything. He was deeply attached to Mr Frank, whom he had known a long time. He said nothing. But then he suddenly asked for his clothing, dressed, and went away. When he came back after dark, he said there was nothing to be seen, that the building looked just as it always had. He had peered into the windows for a while, but everything was deserted and still."

And Henk adds:

"I sat up half the night with Miep, and we discussed back and forth what, if anything, we could possibly do. We also called Mrs Koophuis, but none of us had any ideas, and there was nothing more that we could do in the way of practical activity. I had already called on Mrs Düssel, shortly after noon, in fact. She had suspected nothing, had not even known that her husband had been in Amsterdam all those two years, and so I told her. Now everyone concerned knew about it. At least they *knew*."

CHAPTER 10

Visiting Hours after 9 am

The events that followed were played out in several different theatres.

The ten prisoners were taken to Gestapo headquarters, and locked in a room already containing other arrested persons. Düssel sat in numbed silence. The children whispered to one another. Koophuis sat on the bench beside Mr Frank, who whispered to him:

"You can't imagine how I feel, Koophuis. To think that you are sitting here among us, that we are to blame..."

Koophuis replied dryly:

"Don't give it another thought. It was up to me, and I wouldn't have done it differently."

The interrogation was brief. Horror can develop a routine which on the surface seems identical with standard procedure. Moreover, the case of the ten prisoners was quite clear. Koophuis and Kraler did not attempt to defend themselves; they remained silent, and the officials evidently did not think it worthwhile forcing them to talk. Mr Kraler recalls that the Gestapo man remarked to his typist: "Today was a good day!"

And Kraler thought: Yes, there on the desk he has the gold from Düssel's dental stock, and our radio, and everything they found, and the ten of us to boot.

They were taken away.

Fortunately for Koophuis and Kraler, the year was 1944, not 1943 or 1942. The outcome of the war had already been decided, and although this fact scarcely induced the Gestapo to feel any greater respect for human lives, the future was no longer quite so clear, and in the minds of these officials the first gleams of insecurity were beginning to flicker. They were now rather inclined to stay within the confines of standing orders, instead of making their own decisions. And in cases like those of Kraler and Koophuis the regulations were not entirely clear; and on-the-spot decision was necessary. Therefore, when an international welfare organisation intervened on behalf of Koophuis and pointed out that he was ill, he was released for medical care after a few weeks of imprisonment.

Kraler, too, was not sent to the death camp of Mauthausen, a procedure that would have been virtually automatic only a year earlier. Instead, he went to a camp near Amersfort in Holland, and thence to a forced-labour camp in Zwolle. In March 1945 the inmates of the Zwolle camp were supposed to be removed to Germany. Four hundred men were marched under guard along the highway from Arnhem to Zevenaar. During the march the column was strafed by planes, and in the confusion Kraler and a man from Rotterdam succeeded in escaping. They crawled off into the undergrowth, and when the firing stopped they slipped into a house. After an hour they ventured out again, and hid with a farmer for two days. Travelling by night over side-roads Kraler made his way to Hilversum, where his relatives lived.

As far as the eight Jewish prisoners were concerned, the regulations were completely unequivocal. Their money and valuables had already been taken from them. There was an attempt to make Mr Frank reveal the addresses of other Jews in hiding. He replied that during his twenty-five months in the Secret Annexe he had lost all contact with friends and acquaintances, and therefore knew nothing. This explanation seemed reasonable to the officials, and they sent him back to his cell. A few days later all eight were taken to the railway station and transported to the Westerbork reception camp.

Mr Frank relates:

"We travelled in a regular passenger train. The fact that the door was bolted did not matter very much to us. We were together again, and had been given a little food for the journey. We knew where we were bound, but in spite of that it was almost as if we were once more going travelling, or having an outing, and we were actually cheerful. Cheerful, at least, when I compare this journey with our next. In our hearts, of course, we were already anticipating the possibility that we might not remain in Westerbork to the end. We knew about deportation to Poland, after all. And we also knew what was happening in Auschwitz, Treblinka, and Maidenek. But then, were not the Russians already deep in Poland? The war was so far advanced that we could begin to place a little hope in luck. As we rode toward Westerbork we were hoping our luck would hold. Anne would not move from the window. Outside, it was summer. Meadows, stubble fields, and villages flew by. The telephone wires along the right of way curvetted up and down along the windows. It was like freedom. Can you understand that?"

They do not know what led to their arrest. Mr Frank does not think anyone betrayed them. He is rather inclined to believe that someone who shared the secret may have dropped an incautious remark in the presence of someone he did not know too well.

Mr Koophuis shrugs when he is asked the question. Miep and Henk, too, have no explanation. When asked whether they thought it possible that M, the warehouse clerk, denounced them, they replied shortly:

"He was brought to trial after the war. He denied every accusation, and nothing could be proved against him. We have no idea where he is today."

Elli alone is firmly convinced that M was the one, despite the fact that she, also, has no proof. But little things have lived on in her memory more vividly than in the minds of the others. Nothing she says has been filtered, nothing censored by caution or scruples. She retains everything just as it happened, and careless slips occurred at the time – tiny ones, certainly, but enough for anyone who was on the lookout. For example, Elli says, a good many mornings the pencils would be slightly displaced on the desks, and M used to bustle about the office a good deal more than he had to. Once in a while the feeding bowls for the two warehouse cats would be full in the morning, although they had been left empty in the evening. And it also happened that Mr van Daan once left his briefcase lying on Kraler's desk, and the following morning, when Kraler came to work, M was already there, waiting in the office for him, for they were going to go over some warehouse inventories that day. As they were comparing listings and checking them off, M suddenly asked:

"Is that your briefcase, Mr Kraler?"

Kraler looked up briefly, and replied: "No."

He bent over the list again. But a moment later he looked up once more, and said:

"Why, of course, it is my briefcase. I expect I must have left it here last night."

Twenty-five months are a long time, Elli says, and eight persons are eight individuals. If each one of them committed a single slip each year, that would be sixteen telltale signs. How many would M have needed?

But Mr Frank and his friends do not like to talk about this, and Elli, too, felt easier when I dropped the question. Our fate was as it was, they say, and if someone betrayed us, then it was our fate to be betrayed.

Miep went to the office every day, as S. had ordered. She sat alone in the big building, in utter silence. Only now and then would she hear the two warehouse clerks at work downstairs.

The day after the arrest, S. paid another visit. He looked in on Miep and again threatened to arrest her husband if she disappeared. Then he took the building keys from her and turned them over to M, who had come upstairs with him and waited outside in the corridor. S. went up to the Secret Annexe and stayed there about an hour. Finally Miep saw him leaving, carrying an electric clock which had belonged to the Franks.

The following day Mr D, one of the firm's travelling salesmen, happened to telephone. Miep told him what had happened. That afternoon he called back and advised her to try bribing the police. He had some money saved, he said, which he would contribute. The baker from whom Koophuis had for years been obtaining bread for the group in hiding also wanted to contribute, D said, and there were others who would add to the sum. Only, action would have to be taken quickly, while the prisoners were still in Amsterdam.

Miep telephoned the police and was switched back and forth until she reached S. She said she must talk to him at once. "Come tomorrow morning," S. told her. "We have visiting hours after 9.00am."

Next morning Miep called on S. in his office. There were two or three typists in the room. Seated at his desk, S. asked curtly: "What do you want?"

Miep stepped up to him and asked in a low voice:

"How much?"

No more than those two words.

S. considered for a second. Then he said: "Come back tomorrow. I cannot do anything now. Tomorrow morning around nine o'clock."

But next day, before Miep had a chance to speak, S. said:

"There's nothing to be done; I'm sorry. It used to be possible, but it isn't possible nowadays."

Miep summoned up all her courage and said: "I don't believe you."

Surprisingly, S. did not flare up. He said: "You can see my superior if you like. Go right up."

He told her the number of the superior's room, and Miep went. On the stairs she took a letter from the German affiliate of the firm out of her bag. She decided that she would say she could not answer this letter without Mr Frank and Mr Koophuis.

S.'s superior was rude and brusque. He scarcely took notice of the letter.

"I can do nothing for you."

"Please give the matter your consideration once more," Miep said.

"Get out!"

As Miep came down the stairs, she saw S. standing at the door of his office. He had been waiting for her. He looked into her face and said: "Well? Didn't I tell you? You see – but you wouldn't believe me."

I did not attempt to interview M. Perhaps it would have been possible to locate him. But what could he possibly have replied to my questions? His testimony in court is without interest.

I also did not look for the 'Green policeman'. As far as he is concerned – we will continue to call him S., although his real name is slightly different – my witnesses have told me everything that need be said about him. I shall sum it up once more.

Miep: "He was of medium height and stocky, but not exactly fat. There was something almost genial about him, and, as I have said, he was the kind of man you might meet any day in the street. I think it possible that he might have been capable of a decent act now and then. Incidentally, he wore a wedding ring."

Koophuis: "I was repelled by him. In his way he was a good-natured man. But he had no idea how ill such good-nature became his role, and that was what I found so horrible."

Mr Frank: "Perhaps he would have spared us if he had been by himself."

At which one of the others interposed: "But, you know, he had his orders."

We see, then, that S. scarcely resembled that young SS man who suddenly appeared beside Mrs Düssel's bed, and that he was nothing like the doctor from Münster whom the winds of destiny blew to Auschwitz, where he began to wonder how many doubles he must have in this world.

S. had a million doubles, in type and in fate, so that the doctor's question would scarcely have troubled him, had it ever entered his mind. He was one of those older men who were drafted into civil defence, the police, and ultimately into the home guard, and as a policeman he had been sent into the occupied countries along with many others equally good-natured, equally ordinary fathers of families. I saw so many of them in the photographs at the Rijksinstituut. The Dutch called them 'the Greens', and to this day they have not been forgotten in Amsterdam. But in truth they were altogether ordinary people, and they were put into altogether ordinary German police uniforms. And so, gun in hand, potentially capable of many good deeds but ordered to perform the worst, they fetched Jews from their houses, drove them through the streets, and loaded them into freight cars. On orders.

Miep, Elli, Koophuis, Kraler, Henk, the 'vegetable man on the corner' – they had no orders to do what they did. S. had his orders. What he might have done had he not had them is a useless question. The fact is that he acted under orders, and that is why I did not seek him out. What could I have asked him? Even the generals reply that they were merely obeying orders. What could so ordinary a man possibly have to say?

We others can ask ourselves, however: Did we not receive orders?

And did we not carry them out?

Do we deserve credit for the fact that our orders were more congenial than his?

Or was that only our good fortune?

We do not need S.'s testimony. He was a wholly ordinary person, like all the rest of us. The case is somewhat complicated, however, by the fact that Miep, Elli, Koophuis, Henk, and the vegetable man also maintain that they were wholly ordinary people. We are suddenly forced to raise the question: What is an ordinary person? But S. would in all likelihood have been unable to answer that.

Or should I have asked him: 'Didn't you see that this child was among them?'

No. I did not seek him out.

CHAPTER 11

The Journey into Night

Mrs de Wiek of Apeldoorn tells me: "We had been in Westerbork for three or four weeks when word suddenly went round: 'There are new arrivals.' News of that kind ran like wildfire through the camp, and Judy came running to me, calling: 'New people are coming, Mummy!'

"We dropped everything we were doing and ran to the mustering square, and others came running up from all sides to see the new ones. As we ran we all thought: 'Dear God, let there be none of our friends among them, and none of our relatives.' For although we had not seen friends or relatives for so long, we felt that our misery would only be doubled if we had to share it with them.

"The newcomers were standing in a long row in the mustering square, and one of the clerks was entering their names on the list. We looked at them, and Judy stood beside me, pressing close against me. Fifteen though she was, she was a child among all the grown-up people in the camp, and much as we feared meeting an old friend here, I had sometimes thought: 'Couldn't there be a girl friend for Judy?' And as I looked along the line to see whether there was anyone I knew, I suddenly exclaimed: 'Judy, see!'

"For there in the line stood those eight people whose faces were white as paper, so that you could tell at once that they had been hiding and had not been in the open air for years, and among them was this girl. And I said to Judy: 'Look, Judy, there is a friend for you.'"

It was a Sunday afternoon when I visited Mrs de Wiek in Apeldoorn. The sun shone through the net curtains of her living-room, and there could not have been anything more

Sundayish in all the world than this small-town peace and the June afternoon and the sun sifting through the white curtains.

Mrs de Wiek is a lovely, lively woman who treated me with great friendliness. She now lives alone in Apeldoorn. Her husband was killed, and Judy, who survived to the end of the war working in a munitions factory in Czechoslovakia, is married now, has a child of her own, and lives elsewhere. Mrs de Wiek brushes her hand over the tablecloth, saying: "We must manage somehow to go on…"

I took many notes as she talked.

She, too, had lived in hiding, from April 1943 on. A farmer in Varsseveld, Gelderland, had taken the family in, and the three of them lived in one attic room. When the persecutions of the Jews grew more and more furious, and one round-up followed another in rapid succession, they often spent the night in a hay barn some distance from the farmstead. The farmer would take them there after dark, then clear out the attic room so that no trace of them would be found if the 'Green police' should arrive at night. In the morning he would take them back into the house, and the farmer's wife would give Mrs de Wiek and Judy her own bed until they had warmed up a little.

The de Wieks stayed in hiding for 464 days. The farmer took money only for their food, although he was himself a poor man. Mr de Wiek helped him a little in the barn, very early in the morning, and Judy and Mrs de Wiek knitted and sewed for the farmer's wife and her baby. But they could not do more, for they dared not even show themselves downstairs in the house. They had to hide from visitors, especially from the postman and the midwife, who would drop in often to see the farmer's wife when her second baby was on its way.

They were betrayed by an ex-convict who drifted about

the neighbourhood, spying. On the night of July 16th, 1944, they were taken.

It was a hot night, and they had been sleeping in the attic. The attic window was open, and Mrs de Wiek said she could hear the rustle the cows made as they stirred a little and chewed the cud, in the meadow beside the house. And suddenly she heard a noise on the gravel outside, a noise surely not made by the cows. She woke her husband, and they sat up in bed petrified with fear as someone downstairs shouted:

"Jews, come out of there! Jews, come out of there!" And the butt of a rifle thundered against the front door.

They were taken to the village jail, and next day to the prison in Arnhem. The Gestapo questioned her husband and beat him to make him talk. At the interrogation Mrs de Wiek was told that she and Judy would be sent to Theresienstadt, a 'privileged camp', as it was called, if they would betray the hiding places of other Jews and confess who else helped them apart from the farmer and his wife. Mrs de Wiek's sister was hiding with her children in the same region, and so in her terror she burst out:

"I don't know anything and can't tell you anything even if you beat me to death."

The Gestapo officer answered her:

"We beat no one to death. You know that."

To which she cried:

"Perhaps you don't, but you gas us!"

The officer's eyes narrowed, and he said:

"So you've listened to the atrocity stories on the English radio, too!"

They were held in the Arnhem prison for a week, then sent to Westerbork with twenty-two other prisoners.

At this point Mrs de Wiek interrupted her story, for she

remembered something else that had happened in Arnhem.

There were six or seven of them in the cell, all women. One day one of the women saw a group of workmen in the street outside. She took a scrap of paper and wrote on it in big block letters: NEWS? and held the paper against the window pane. The workmen understood what she meant. They left, and returned in the evening carrying a large board. On it was written:

ATTEMPTED ASSASSINATION OF HITLER – REVOLUTION IN GERMANY

The women threw their arms around one another and wept for joy. The day was July 20th, 1944.

But four days later they were taken to Westerbork camp in Drenths province, for the uprising in Berlin had collapsed.

Mrs de Wiek says:

"I saw Anne Frank and Peter van Daan every day in Westerbork. They were always together, and I often said to my husband: 'Look at those two beautiful young people…'

"In Westerbork Anne was lovely, so radiant that her beauty flowed over into Peter. She was very pallid at first, but there was something so intensely attractive about her frailty and her expressive face that at first Judy was too shy to make friends with her.

"Perhaps it's not the right expression to say that Anne's eyes were radiant. But they had a glow, if you know what I mean. And her movements, her looks, had such a lilt to them that I often asked myself: Can she possibly be happy?

"She was happy in Westerbork, though that seems almost incredible, for things were hard for us in the camp. We 'convict Jews', who had been arrested in hiding places, were treated even more harshly than the others. We had to wear blue overalls with a red bib, and wooden shoes, while the others were allowed to keep their own clothing; and our men had their heads shaved. Three hundred persons lived in each barracks. We were sent to work at five in the morning, the children to the cable workshop and we grown-ups to a shed where we had to break up old batteries and salvage the parts. The metal parts and the carbon rods were collected, and sent somewhere to be made into new batteries. The food was bad, we were always kept on the run, and in spite of that all we ever heard was: Faster, faster! But Anne was happy; it was as if she were liberated, for now she could see new people and talk to them, and could laugh, while I could think of nothing but: Will they send us to Poland? Will we live through it?

"Roll call was the worst time for me. We often waited for more than an hour, row upon row of fives filling the whole of the big square, and I couldn't help looking at our shoes all the time. These were the wooden shoes which had been thrown to us on arrival, irrespective of size, so that we all had sore feet; and among these were the newcomers' shoes, still in good shape; and then the shoes of those who had already been here half a year; in tatters, coming apart at the soles, or mere rags held together with string. I could not help looking at our shoes as we stood there, row upon row, and it occurred to me that when misery comes it creeps up from below...

"You ask me what Anne's mother was like? There in Westerbork she was quiet; she seemed numbed all the time, and I did not know her before the camp. She no longer talked very much. Margot, too, spoke little, but Edith Frank could have been a mute. She said nothing at work, and in the evenings she was always washing underclothing. The water was murky and there was no soap, but she went on washing, all the time.

"Anne's father was quiet, too, but it was a reassuring quietness that helped Anne and helped the rest of us, too. He lived in the men's barracks, but once when Anne was sick he came over to visit her every evening and would stand beside her bed for hours, telling her stories. Anne was so like him that when she recovered and David fell ill, a twelve-year-old boy who lived in the women's barracks with us, she acted in just the same way, stood by his bed and talked to him. David came from an orthodox family, and he and Anne always talked about God. As for God – I often thought in those days: God… But when I saw the two children together, I thought: No, I must not have such thoughts.

"That was in Westerbork. Anne was happy there, although we weren't in safety nor at the end of our misery. For most of us that was not yet the last stage, but the one before the last, or the one before that. At the time we did not really know what the end was, but we knew we were not safe, and we were afraid.

"Sometimes we heard news from the outside world. I don't know how the news reached the camp, for there was no radio; but there were whispers in the barracks all the time. At the end of August we heard that Paris had already fallen. And on September 3rd Brussels fell, and on the 4th Antwerp, and a week later the Americans reached the German border near Aachen. But by then there was no more chance of our being saved. We were already on the move.

"On September 2nd we were told that a thousand persons would leave in the morning. We were among them, and the Franks, the van Daans, Mr Düssel – everybody I knew. Later we learned that this was the very last shipment to leave Holland.

"During the night we packed up the few things we had

156

been allowed to keep. Someone had a little ink, and with that we marked our names on the blankets we were to take with us, and we made the children repeat again and again the addresses where we were to meet after the war, in case we were separated. I again gave Judy the address of her aunt in Zutphen, and the Franks had agreed on an address in Switzerland.

"It was a long freight train. We were driven like cattle to the railway platform, and seventy-five persons were bundled into each truck. The trucks were closed tight; there was only one small barred window high up.

"When the train stopped for the first time, we were already in Germany. Some bread and a pail of beet marmalade were tossed into the truck. We did not know where we were, since the train had not stopped at a station, but at a siding, and we could not ask because SS guards were patrolling up and down outside the train.

"We stopped many times in the open country, somewhere or other, and once the train suddenly started backing, so that someone cried: 'Look, we're going back to Holland!'

"But we did not go to Holland. We went back and forth but deeper and deeper into Germany, past plough-lands and stubble fields across Germany. Now and then when the train stopped, the SS men came to the door and held out their caps, and we were supposed to put our money and valuables into the caps. Some of us actually had a few things left, sewed into our clothes, for instance, and there were some who took out what they had, flung it into the SS caps, and then the train went on. That was how it went, night and day, and night again.

"The children had got together in the truck, and we could hear them talking, but we in our corner were silent. The children would also pull themselves up on the bars at times and peer through the small window. Anne and Judy did this, and reported that it was raining outside. Anne was riding through the country of her birth, but it might as well have been Brazil or Asia, for even when they were able to read the name of a station as it flitted by outside, the name meant nothing to us; the place was only a small village. All we did know was that we were headed east.

"As I say, we adults were silent. At most we would ask the children once again whether they still remembered the addresses, nothing more.

"I sat beside my husband on a small box. The box swayed every time the wheels jolted against the rails. When the third day came and we had not yet arrived, my husband took my hand and suddenly said: 'I want to thank you for the wonderful life we have had together.'

"I snatched my hand away from him, crying: 'What are you thinking of? It's not over!'

"But he calmly reached for my hand again, and took it, and repeated several times: 'I thank you. Thank you for the life we have had.'

"Then I left my hand in his and did not try to draw it away.

"On the third night the train suddenly came to a stop. The doors of the truck were slid violently open, and the first we saw of Auschwitz were the glaring searchlights fixed on the train, and outside on the platform men were running back and forth as though they were crazy to show how hard they were working. Those were the Kapos, whom we would soon get to know. Behind them, at the rear of the platform, stood the SS officers. They could be seen distinctly against the light. They were trimly built and smartly dressed, and had big dogs at their sides. As I watched, one of them stooped and patted his dog. The SS men who had accompanied our train went over to them. Now they wore their caps, which they had used to make collections from truck to truck, neatly at the prescribed angle on their heads.

"But all that was only a moment's glimpse, for now people began pouring out of the train, thronging the platform, and the Kapos[5] shouted: 'Faster, faster!' And then a loudspeaker drowned out all the voices, roaring:

"'Women to the left! Men to the right!'

"I saw them as they went away, Mr van Daan and Mr Düssel and Peter and Mr Frank, all of them being driven to the right. But I saw no sign of my husband. He had suddenly vanished.

"'Listen!' the loudspeaker bawled again. 'It is an hour's march to the women's camp. For children and the sick there are lorries waiting at the end of the platform.'

"We could see the lorries; they were painted with big red crosses. But we had no chance to reach them, we could see that at once, for everyone made a rush for them – and who among us was not sick and done in after those days on the train? Knots of people were still hanging on to them as they started off. No one had put a stop to the far too many who were crowding in. But the lorries did not go very far. Not one of those who went along on the lorries ever arrived at the women's camp, and no one ever found any trace of them.

"When we reached the Auschwitz-Birkenau women's camp, we were assigned to Block 29. That night march had been frightful. They had hustled us along at a brutal pace, but one woman helped the other, and so none fell behind. After we reached the barracks I could not help thinking: How is it that not a single one of us threw herself down on the ground and let herself be trampled to death or shot?

---

[5] Kapos were prisoners, usually drawn from the criminal element, to whom the SS assigned positions of authority. Many of them were noted for emulating their masters in cruelty.

"Today the whole world knows what Auschwitz was. But scarcely anyone knows where it was situated, and that the place and the camp still exist. Everyone acts as though it were on the moon, or at any rate not in this world. And when I say to people: 'Do you know that it was not thirty miles away from Gleiwitz and Hindenburg, two big German cities?' they say: 'Didn't anyone in those cities realise?' God only knows whether anyone did.

"We stayed together – that much good fortune we still had. Perhaps that is why we endured longer than the others, who were all alone. People of every language and country were gathered in those barracks. And we now began to see that misery is not doubled when it is shared.

"I remained together with Judy until she was taken into Czechoslovakia on October 27th, and with Margot and Anne Frank until they disappeared, three days after July, and with Mrs Frank until she died on January 6th, 1945. Ten days later the SS guards fled from the camp. Mrs van Daan was the only one I did not see again in Block 29 or in the camp. I lost sight of her the moment we arrived. And the only one of the men I saw again was Mr Frank, but by then the Russians had liberated us and we were being cared for in a school in Kattowitz. Mr Frank was sitting alone at a long table when I came in and we recognised each other. I said to him:

"'I know nothing about the children. They were taken away.'

"After a while I told him that his wife had died, in bed, right beside me. Mr Frank did not move when I told him. I looked into his face, but he had turned away, and then he made a movement. I no longer remember exactly what it was, but it seems to me he laid his head on the table."

*

Mrs de Wiek speaks good German, for she was in Germany as a child, and for a while went to school there. She scarcely ever makes an error in German, but now and then she uses an uncommon word. Occasionally the word is a Dutch one, but does not seem foreign in the German sentence, only new and as if fresh from the mint. Thus she told me about one night when there was a fire in the camp. She now believes it was the night that the death squads among the prisoners set fire to Crematorium III and the gas chambers, and attempted to revolt – that was the night of October 6th. At the time the other prisoners did not know what was burning. They could only see, above the roof of the neighbouring barracks, the tall, rushing flames against the night sky, and all the women and children threw themselves to the floor, praying in their various languages, each to his own God, that no wind would come up and no sparks fall upon their roof, for if it caught fire they would all burn to death, locked in as they were. And whatever God was in the barracks heard their plea: no wind blew up and no sparks fell on the roof, for the air was *bladstil* (still as a leaf).

Mrs de Wiek noticed my reaction.

"Isn't that a German word?" she asked.

"Yes, it is a German word," I replied. "*Blatt-still* – I see just what you mean."

Sometimes, too, she used words that were neither new nor unusual, but they took on a newly minted sound as she spoke them.

"I wanted and wanted to stay alive," she said, "but in the end I, too, fell ill. I was sent to the hospital barracks, and there I saw Mrs Frank again. I lay down beside her. She was very weak and no longer eating, scarcely in her right mind. Whatever food she was given she collected under her blanket, saying that she was saving it for her husband, because he needed it – and then the bread spoiled under the blanket.

161

"I don't know whether she was so weakened because she was starving, or whether she had stopped eating because she was too weak to eat. There was no longer any way of telling. I watched her die, without a murmur, and I thought: Now I will die, too. But the Polish woman doctor in the barracks said to me: 'You will pull through. You still have your face.'"

This was an exact quotation, Mrs de Wiek said, and she was still wondering what the Polish doctor had meant. She had not fathomed it, and wanted to know whether I could.

But I did not tell her that I did.

I have seen photographs of the round-ups and the arrests and the shipments of prisoners, and photographs of the concentration camps. And I saw that many of the victims gave up the moment they were arrested, and lost their faces. They were photographed that way by the propaganda reporters – photographed in the street, at the collecting points. They stood with drooping heads, or with arms lifted on order, and among the onlookers were the vile ones who said: "Look at those animals!"

Some of them really had faces that were no longer human. That was what had been done to them. Among the concentration-camp inmates they were called 'the Mussulmen'.[6] But in reality they looked like garrotted angels, and no longer belonged to this world. They were already on the way back, with their grey, emaciated faces and their sallow, translucent skin. I think now that angels are grey and emaciated, and their wings are only something our imaginations have added.

Mrs de Wiek's face has remained almost unseared. Only

[6] Prisoners characterised as Mussulmen remain between life and death, without expressing emotional reactions in the extreme phase of starvation. A deep somatic and emotional stigma remains in those who survived the Mussulmen state.

when she smiles is there a shadow around her mouth, and she smiles very often. She says:

"I don't know whether I am using the term correctly, but I might say, for example, that Anne still had her face, up to the last. Actually she seemed to me in Auschwitz even more beautiful than in Westerbork, although she now no longer had her long hair. On our arrival our heads had been shaved; they needed women's hair – for power belting and pipe-joint packing in U-boats, I think. But now you could see that her beauty was wholly in her eyes, in her eyes alone, which seemed to grow bigger the thinner she became. Her gaiety had vanished, but she was still lively and sweet, and with her charm she sometimes secured things that the rest of us had long since given up hoping for.

"For example, we had no clothing apart from a grey sack, and under that we were naked. But when the weather turned cold, Anne came into the barracks one day wearing a suit of men's long underwear. She had begged it somewhere. She looked screamingly funny with those long white legs, but somehow still charming.

"We were divided into groups of five for roll call, work, and distribution of food. You see, we had only one cup to each group of five. Anne was the youngest in her group, but nevertheless she was the leader of it. She also distributed the bread in the barracks, and she did it so well and fairly that there was none of the usual grumbling.

"Here is another example. We were always thirsty, so thirsty that at roll call we would stick out our tongues if it happened to be raining or snowing, and many became sick from bad water. But the thirst was worse than any sickness. And once, when I was so far gone that I almost died because there was nothing to drink, Anne suddenly came to me with a cup of coffee. To this day I don't know where she got it.

"She, too, was the one who saw to the last what was going

163

on all around us. We had long since stopped seeing. Who bothered to look when the flames shot up into the sky from the crematoria at night? Or when in the neighbouring barracks they suddenly ordered, 'Block closed', and we knew that now people were being selected and gassed? It scarcely troubled us – we were beyond feelings. We scurried when the Kapos shouted their everlasting 'Faster, faster!' We dug up sods of grass, twelve hours in succession, although the sods were no longer of any use because the Russians were coming closer day by day, and all we did was to toss the sods in a heap; but they drove us on and we dug out the sods and put up no resistance, not even in thought any more. *They* did not care how many died at work, and we scarcely cared either. The principal thing was that we brought the dead back, so that the count would be in order.

"We scarcely saw and heard these things any longer. Something protected us, kept us from seeing. But Anne had no such protection, to the last. I can still see her standing at the door and looking down the camp street as a herd of naked gypsy girls was driven by, to the crematorium, and Anne watched them going and cried. And she cried also when we marched past the Hungarian children who had already been waiting half a day in the rain in front of the gas chambers, because it was not yet their turn. And Anne nudged me, and said: 'Look, look. Their eyes…'

"She cried. And you cannot imagine how soon most of us came to the end of our tears.

"Later they gassed only the sick, the ones whose cases were quite hopeless, for the Russians were now so close that they might reach us in a single advance. Word went around the camp that the SS were beginning to hide the traces of what they had done. I began to hope again, for if the Russians came soon enough…

"Then Judy was taken away. It happened very fast. There was the sudden cry of 'Block closed!' and we all had to undress and pass by an SS doctor, who picked out the youngest and strongest for a munitions factory in Czechoslovakia. Judy was one of the first taken, and Anne and Margot would certainly have gone also, and survived, except that they had scabies and the doctor rejected them.

"That was on October 27th. On October 30th there was another 'selection'. The block was closed again, but this time we had to wait naked on the mustering ground, and it took a long time. Then we had to file singly, one behind the other, into the barracks, and inside a searchlight was set up. There stood the doctor, and we had to step into the light. By this time we saw that he picked out a great many who were not too sick or old, and then we knew that they would escape and that the old and sick would be gassed after all.

"In front of us stood a woman who was sixty, but she said she was forty and she was allowed to go along to Belsen.

"Then it was my turn, and I, too, made myself ten years younger. I called out to the doctor: 'I am twenty-nine. And I have never had dysentery yet.'

"But he jerked his thumb and sent me to join the old and sick.

"Then came Mrs Frank – and she, too, joined our group at once.

"Then it was the turn of the two girls, Anne and Margot. Even under the glare of that searchlight Anne still had her face, and she encouraged Margot, and Margot walked erect into the light. There they stood for a moment, naked and shaven-headed, and Anne looked over at us with her unclouded face, looked straight and stood straight, and then they went on. We could not see what was on the other side of the searchlight. Mrs Frank screamed: 'The children! Oh God…'

*

"Now imagine this:

"The barracks door stood open. We thronged toward the door. Close by, the camp fence could be seen, and the latticework of electric wire. Many women were drooped against it, dead. It was only a short leap to it. But we did not take the leap. We let ourselves be driven into a barracks that was called 'the scabies barracks'. There was no light inside, and we stumbled over one another and fell.

"Mrs Frank lay beside me, clutching my hand tightly. Suddenly someone wrenched open the door and a Greek woman came rushing in – she was senior orderly in one of the barracks. She pulled away the three women who had lain on top of the heap, and then Mrs Frank and myself, and a moment later the five of us were standing in the mustering square with women from a different block. The Greek woman whispered to us: 'Quiet, they won't notice. Some of our people are missing.'

"Then the count began, and as the SS man walked past us, counting the groups of five, the trucks drove up in front of the scabies barracks and they took the women out.

"But Mrs Frank died anyway, later. And my husband died, too. Mr Frank told me that, when we met again in Kattowitz. Mr van Daan was gassed. Mr Frank saw him marching to the gas chamber. Mr Düssel was sent back to Germany, and died in Neuengamme. Peter was taken along by the SS when they left Auschwitz in January. Mr Frank was in the infirmary at the time, and he had tried to persuade Peter to hide in the infirmary also, but Peter did not dare.

"So they took Peter with them. They took along all who could still walk on that great trek, even the one or two hundred dwarfs from Hungary who had been in the camp for ages. The SS had kept them from being gassed because the dwarfs amused them. Now they took them along. It was cold, and the roads covered with ice. Most of them were never heard of again. Peter van Daan was among these. Many of the SS men from Auschwitz disappeared also. No one knows, for example, where Dr Mengele is, whether he died or is still living somewhere. Dr Mengele was the doctor who stood by the searchlight during the 'selections' sending some of us to the right and some to the left."

CHAPTER 12

The End of the Trail and the Moss

Mrs Renate L A, who now lives in London, says:

"I did not know Anne Frank, although I, too, was transported from Auschwitz to Belsen in October 1944, together with my sister, and possibly in the same cattle car. We spoke German, and she understood it, and in Belsen there were comparatively few left who understood German. It is even possible that we lived and slept in the same barrack, perhaps even on the same straw pallet at night. But do you think anyone in Belsen asked anyone else: 'Who are you?' Identity no longer existed there. There was only horror and confusion, and to be alive oneself was an almost superhuman effort. But I can tell you how a person of fifteen or sixteen felt in Belsen, for my sister and I were both Anne's age – only we had perhaps a longer taste of camp. We were not taken so late as the summer of 1944. At the very beginning of the war we had been pressed into garbage collection work in Breslau, and then sent to the forced-labour camp of the Sacrau paper factory, because our father was a Jewish lawyer and we had not left Germany in time. In 1940 we were sent to prison and then to the penitentiary because we had helped French prisoners of war to escape from the paper factory, and then in 1942 we were shipped to Auschwitz when they were clearing out the penitentiaries for new prisoners. Our experience helped us a great deal. And, you see, we already had been through typhus. We had had it in Auschwitz. But this must be said: In Auschwitz a person could live – until he was put to death. But in Belsen it was impossible to live even that long.

"We were en route for days. The train stopped at every second station because of some air raid. Then it would advance a short distance and stop again. After an hour's standstill it would go on for another half hour. We almost died of hunger.

"When our train arrived in Belsen, the SS were waiting on the platform for us, with fixed bayonets. We had to leave the dead lying in the trucks and line up in marching order. Then we started. The way led for a long distance through the woods. We kept asking ourselves: What will it be like? But we could see nothing but forest to either side, and on the edges of the road stood signposts with death's-heads and the warning that civilians were forbidden to enter this area. One sign read: TO THE FIRING RANGE.

"We passed through the barbed-wire gate of the camp without really noticing it, for there was no trace of any camp. No barracks, no crematorium, no dogs, and suddenly the SS, too, was gone, for the soldiers who had driven us along remained behind at the gate.

"There we stood and looked around in astonishment. But soon some curious prisoners came towards us out of the wasteland. Their heads were shaved and they looked in a very bad way.

"'Where does one live here?' I asked a woman. 'In tents,' she told me. 'We all sleep on the ground.' 'And is there water here?' 'Not much.' 'Latrines?' 'We have just made a pit for ourselves.' 'And the food?' 'Irregular, little of it, and bad.'

"We knew what questions to ask when we arrived in a new camp – we had had plenty of camp life, you see. But there was little need to ask many questions. The indications were clear enough. After my first half hour in Belsen I ran across a woman whom I had known at Auschwitz. She had been block orderly there, and had had decent clothing and food. Now here she stood holding a soup kettle, scraping it out and greedily licking the dregs. When I saw that, I knew enough. It was a bad camp where not even the privileged group had enough to eat. My sister and I looked at one another, and my sister, who had just turned sixteen, said: 'No one will come out of this camp alive.'

"She was not far wrong.

"The cluster of tents looked quite jolly from a distance, like a huge circus in the midst of the Lüneburg heath, and all around it were the forest and the heath, beautiful as blue velvet. But the third night I was there we had a storm. The tents ripped and flew off, and the heavy poles came crashing down on us. The next two nights we slept in a storage shed, among heaps of SS caps and military boots. On the third day we were driven to a block of barracks that had meanwhile been cleared. That was the beginning of our stay in Belsen.

"We did not have to work there, at least not in the early days. Later we had to transport the dead. There were no carts. We were given strips of bandage with which we tied together their arms and legs and then we dragged the bodies to the cremation ground, where they were piled up, a layer of corpses and then a layer of railway sleepers, and petrol was poured on top of this. But in the beginning we just lay around waiting to see whether there would be anything to eat. There rarely was, and we became more and more run-down.

"Understand me rightly: Auschwitz had been a fantastically well-organised, spick-and-span hell. The food was bad, but it was distributed regularly. We had kept our barracks so clean that you could have eaten off the floor. Anyone who died in the barracks was taken away first thing in the morning. Anyone who fell ill disappeared also. Those who were gassed did not scream. They just were no longer there. The crematoria smoked, but we received our rations and had roll calls. The SS harassed us at roll call and kept guard with machine guns from the watchtowers, and the camp fences were charged with high-tension electricity, but we could wash every day and sometimes even take showers. If you could forget the gas chambers, you could manage to live.

"In Belsen it was different. We scarcely saw the SS guards. There were no roll calls and no order, nothing but the heath and hunger and people as fluttery from starvation as a flock of chickens, and there was neither food nor water nor hope, for it no longer meant anything to us that the Allies had reached the Rhine. We had typhus in the camp, and it was said that before the Allies came the SS would blow us all up."

Lies P told the journalists in Jerusalem:

"I had seen Anne in school for the last time on the Thursday or Friday before she disappeared. That week Mrs Frank had borrowed a kitchen balance from us, and on Monday my mother sent me over to the Franks for the balance because she suddenly needed it for something.

"I went across the street and rang the Franks' bell, but I had to ring for a long time before Mr Goudsmit, with whom the Franks lived, opened the door. I asked: 'Isn't anybody at home, Mr Goudsmit?'

"Mr Goudsmit thought for a second. Then he said: 'Listen, Lies, the Franks are no longer here.' And he told me that some time ago a German Army officer had come to see Mr Frank; it was a friend from the First War, and they had talked together for a long time, and now this officer had smuggled the Franks across the border – to Switzerland, Mr Goudsmit guessed. So I went home, thinking: 'Now you'll never see her again.'"

Lies and her parents did not go into hiding, for Lies's mother was expecting a baby at the time. Relations in Switzerland had obtained South American passports for the family, so that they could hope to remain unmolested. But in spite of their passports they were sent to Westerbork in 1943, and later to the Belsen concentration camp. There they lived in a block 'for neutral foreigners'. They were occasionally permitted to receive a Red Cross parcel, but Lies's mother died, and her father, too, fell ill and died during the winter of 1944–45.

That same winter Lies one day heard that in the next block of the camp, which was separated from hers by a barbed-wire fence, a group from Auschwitz had arrived, among them Margot and Anne Frank.

Lies said to the reporters:

"I waited until night. Then I stole out of the barrack, went over to the barbed wire, and called softly into the darkness: 'Is anyone over there?'

A voice answered: 'I am here. I am Mrs van Daan.'

"We had known the van Daans in Amsterdam. I told her who I was, and asked whether Margot or Anne could come to the fence. Mrs van Daan answered in a breathless voice that Margot was ill, but that Anne could probably come, and she would go to look for her.

"I waited, shivering in the darkness. It took a long time. But suddenly I heard a voice: 'Lies, Lies? Where are you?'

"It was Anne, and I ran in the direction of the voice, and then I saw her beyond the barbed wire. She was in rags. I saw her emaciated, sunken face in the darkness. Her eyes were very large. We cried and cried, for now there was only the barbed wire between us, nothing more. And no longer any difference in our fates.

"I told Anne that my mother had died and my father was dying, and Anne told me that she knew nothing about her father, but that her mother had stayed behind in Auschwitz. Only Margot was still with her, but she was already very ill. They had met Mrs van Daan again only after their arrival here in Belsen.

"But there was a difference between us, after all. I was in a block where we still occasionally had parcels. Anne had nothing at all. She was freezing, and starving. I called to her in a whisper:

" 'I'll see what I can do, Anne. Maybe… Come back here tomorrow, will you?'

"And Anne called across: 'Yes, tomorrow. I'll come.' "

Mrs B of Amsterdam, who met Anne in Westerbork, states:

"In November 1944 I met her again with her sister in Bergen-Belsen. We lived in the same block and saw each other often. We also celebrated Christmas together. We had saved some stale bread, and we cut this into tiny pieces and put onions and boiled cabbage on the pieces. By 'we' I mean the Daniels sisters, my sister and myself, and Margot and Anne. Over our feast we nearly forgot our misery, for a few hours. We were almost happy. Yes, I know that it sounds ghastly now, but we really were a little happy for a few hours, in spite of everything."

Mrs L, the mother of Trees L, tells me:

"Yes, I saw Anne in Belsen. She had come with a trainload from Auschwitz, and at first they were put up in tents because there was no room in the barracks. But when the weather turned and autumn came to the heath, the wind tore up these tents one night, and knocked them over. Then Anne and the others were distributed among the various blocks, and Margot and Anne were placed in the block adjoining ours. I could see Anne beyond the barbed wire across the camp street. Over there conditions were even worse than they were among us, for we still received an occasional parcel while they had nothing at all. So I called across the street:

" 'Don't go away, Anne. Wait!'

"And I ran into the barrack and packed up whatever I could find, packed it into a bundle and ran back to the barbed wire. But it was so far across to the other block, and we women were so weak. While we were wondering how we could throw the bundle across, Mr Brill came by. Mr Brill lived with us. He was very tall, and I said to him: 'I have an old dress here, and soap and a piece of bread, Mr Brill. Please throw it across. You see the child, standing over there.'

"Mr Brill hesitated at first, not certain whether it was safe, because the guard could see us. But he overcame his fears at the sight of her. Seeing her overcame all our fears. So he took the bundle and flung his arm far back and then sent it flying in a high arc across to the other side."

But at this moment Mrs L interrupted herself. She looked at me, and said suddenly in a bitter voice:

"Why am I telling you all this? What does it matter to you? A friend of mine was in Germany last year, and she wrote to me from Freiburg: 'The people of Freiburg say it is not true. They know nothing and want to know nothing. They want to put it all behind them.' What is the use of my going over it?"

But then she went on. The thing itself spoke out of her. Her husband sat close by, and Trees also. But they were no longer addressing me, they were addressing one another. It was as if I had been shut out of the conversation. Trees said to her mother: "Do you remember how…?" And her mother nodded and asked in turn: "Do you remember how…?"

Only Mr L sat very still. He did not say a word. He is in his sixties, I imagine, and has a handsome, narrow, very Jewish head, like the head of King David as painted by Chagall. He has a sparse beard. His eyes, under the high arches of his eyebrows and furrowed forehead, lie large and weary in their sockets, surrounded with the tracery imprinted by fate.

The women talk on, not directing their speech to me at all, and with heavy heart I listen to what they say. They mention the names of camps; they speak of trains of cattle trucks headed they knew not where. Words fall, like 'firing squad', and that most frightful word of all: 'selection'. The years waver past – and these are *our* times they are speaking of, and *our* country; and those who speak are human beings in Central Europe. They are speaking of the days of their lives. Mrs L glances at me only once, and her look seems to ask: 'What is the use of your writing a book about it?'

I drove from Amsterdam to Belsen and spent a day walking over the heath with a friend. Early in the morning we talked by telephone with a man in Celle. We asked him for the names of persons who might still know something about the concentration-camp days. He gave us addresses, but added: "There's no point in it. You will come up against a stone wall. You'll see, no one will know anything."

He proved wrong. People kept silent, and silence lay like a coat of enamel over the whole vicinity. But it was a simple matter to break through the enamel; there was no need for stratagems; and I now feel that this silence must be broken. For it is no longer mere silence; it is a trauma.

We spoke with three persons that day: with a woman who for years has been writing a 'district chronicle', as she called it: with a retired town official now living in a nearby village, and with a man from Bergen. Of these three, only one refused to speak. One of three. Two out of three did not 'put it behind' them. There is no getting away from it. And when we took leave of each other, toward evening, my friend said: "We still have a chance." For two out of three had spoken, and as we left them we could see that they were glad, or at least somewhat eased.

*

What the 'chronicler' said was brief enough.

"I went about all the villages in the district after the war," she declared, "and I can assure you that nobody knew anything. It was all kept so secret, you see. I was living here in the region at the time too. Until 1945 I was editor of a newspaper, and even I knew nothing whatsoever about the camp."

For our second visit we called on Mr R, the retired official. The first thing he asked was:

"Have you come by car?"

"Yes."

"Then let us drive over there. It is only half an hour's ride."

We drove out into the Belsen heath. On the way R told us that he had seen the camp before British engineers burned it down with flamethrowers, for he belonged to the group of German officials who had made a compulsory tour of the camp under orders of the British commander. R said:

"The barracks were still standing then, and the mass graves were still open. Every day a few hundred persons were still dying of typhus and typhoid fever and debilitation. A good many died simply because they could no longer grasp the fact that they had been liberated.

"There had been a great deal of typhus here. But most of the victims had simply starved to death. Transportation was no longer functioning. I know that even Kramer drove around the district and complained to the authorities, but he received no food supplies from them. Kramer was the SS commander of the camp. The supply organisation simply stopped functioning during the last months. The railways had been bombed. The roads were blocked..." After a moment, R added in a lower voice:

"Nevertheless, they continued to bring people here, trainfuls of them, every day, right up to the last. There was always room on the rails for the cattle trucks... And as we were standing there, by these pits full of the dead, the Britisher asked us whether we had known. I don't know what the others replied. I said I did know. I had seen the freight trucks, after all. And I had reported to my superiors what I had seen, and what people were saying. The British had only to look in my office. I had copies of the reports in my desk drawers, after all. But if they had asked: 'Where are the replies?' I would have had to tell them: 'No reply ever came. Not a word...'"

R showed us first the cemetery in the woods where 50,000 Russian prisoners of war are buried, who died here in 1941. Next to them is a cemetery for Italians. There are supposed to be 300 or 3,000 – no one knows exactly.

From the Russian cemetery it is only a mile or so to the Belsen camp. The road leads through thickets and tall, whispering firs. It was June; lupins were in flower in the scrubland, and we could hear the cuckoo.

Above the mass graves shallow mounds rise, grown over with heath grass. A few have been planted with knee-high dwarf pines. Boards bearing the number of the dead stand beside the mounds. But there are graves here marked by neither mounds nor signboards, for before the British reached the camp the SS burned the dead or buried them higgledy-piggledy. At least 30,000 persons died in the camp.

R led us to where the barracks had stood. Now birches and pines are growing there. The birches are not much higher than a man's reach, but they are already making that same tacky, slow, June stir as the tall birch in Frankfurt, on Marbachweg. The sound here is much stronger, for the wind comes in long waves across the heath, and the rustle follows in its wake like the gigantic train of a dress.

Amid the low growth of pines and birches many large, rectangular places can be seen on the surface of the heath. I paced one off. It measured fifteen by forty paces. Some are smaller, some larger. R told me that these were the sites of the barracks. Although they were burned down twelve years ago, grass grows slowly on the heath, and the tracks of bare feet between the barracks have not yet been erased. All around is heath and grass. But on these rectangular spots there is only a luxuriant growth of shaggy moss. In June it is of a rust-red colour.

Mr R introduced us to Mr K, and so we had our third conversation, towards evening. We sat on the edge of the big highway that passes by Bergen. It was a warm evening. The trailer lorries coursed down Federal Highway No 3, which goes from Buxtehude to Basel; they made such a rumble that sometimes we had almost to shout to hear each other.

K is an elderly man now, but he still has an unlined, vigorous, sun-tanned face. He formerly lived in Bergen, which is but a few miles from Belsen.

K said:

"The first I heard of it all was a telephone call. Someone in an SS headquarters twenty-five miles from Bergen called the Bergen police and said a train had passed through and had stopped briefly in their district, and that now sixteen dead persons were lying on the railway embankment. He wanted the Bergen police to come and remove the dead. But the police would not take them.

"That was the beginning. Later on, some of the SS men would come into town, and I heard that a young SS man had visited police headquarters in Bergen and inquired whether there were any chance of his transferring to the police. He said he could no longer stand it, over there in the camp.

"A few days after that I met an SS girl in uniform in the street. They had girls in the SS too, you know. She might have been eighteen, or at most twenty, and was walking alone. I tried to strike up a conversation with her about it. But she only said: 'That is none of your business. We are attending to it. It is our affair.'

"But it was no longer simply their affair, because we could see the trains passing through, and by now they were coming by day as well as night. Some of the trains had roofless trucks, the sides reaching just about chest-high, and people were packed into them like… like pit-props."

As Mr K said this his face was no longer smooth, but seamed and tormented. He went on, and we listened in silence:

"I once dropped into an inn, out in the country, and ordered a glass of beer. That was in March. The woman at the bar pushed the beer across the counter to me. It wasn't until I was on the point of drinking that I noticed the stench in the place. I sniffed the air and realised that the smell was awful, and I asked the woman: 'What is that stench?' She said to me: 'Oh, be quiet! The window was open for a while, and over there…' She pointed through the now closed window toward Belsen. 'Over there they're burning some more; they've been at it again all day.'

"Then I thought: I have to see this. I took my bicycle and rode over to Belsen, to the platform where the railway line ended. A train was standing there. The SS guards shouted: 'Move on, move on!' I walked a few steps, pushing the bicycle; but they were busy with the train, and so I stopped again. There were other onlookers, and we saw them driving the people out on the platform. The dead remained behind in the trucks, and then they threw these on a heap. But the ones who could still walk were driven across the platform and down the road. I saw two young Jews helping an old man. They supported him and led him down the road, his feet shuffling slowly through the sand. He looked like a priest – for he had a long white beard – or like a prophet. His head hung back, so that his eyes were staring at the sky. The two boys guided him, their eyes on his face, and so they did not notice that his feet stopped moving. Otherwise there was no change in him; it was only that his feet were now dragging in the sand. And they supported and carried the dead man until he suddenly slumped forward. Then the SS guards shouted again: 'Move on!' I did not realise that they meant me until one of them came running towards me. Then I mounted my bicycle and rode off."

That was how they perished.

How Mrs van Daan died is not known. Margot, Mrs B says, died at the end of February or the beginning of March. She had been gravely ill, in a profound coma for days. While unconscious she had fallen out of bed, and was dead when her friends tried to lift her back. "Anne, who was already ill at the time, was not informed of her sister's death; but after a few days she sensed it, and soon afterwards she died, peacefully, feeling that nothing bad was happening to her."

Lies P told the reporters in Jerusalem:

"I saw Anne again, for she came to the fence on the following night. I had packed up a woollen jacket and some biscuits and sugar and a tin of sardines for her. I called out: 'Anne, watch now!' Then I threw the bundle across. But I heard only screams and Anne crying, and I shouted: 'Anne, what's happened?' And she called back, weeping 'A woman caught it and won't give it to me.' Then I heard rapid footsteps as the woman ran away. I said: 'Anne, come again. I'll see what else I can find…' Next time I had only a pair of stockings and biscuits, but this time she caught it.'"

Lies also informed the reporters:

"I was told that she died of typhus, but I myself did not see her after that February night, for I did not stay in Belsen. I was sent out in a trainload destined for Theresienstadt, but our train ran right into the middle of a Russian offensive, and the Russians liberated us."

Renate L A says:

"In Auschwitz we had had visible enemies: the gas chambers, the SS, the brutality. But in Belsen we were left to ourselves. There we had not even hatred to buoy us up. We had only ourselves and our filthy bodies; we had only thirst, hunger, and the dead, the corpses lying all around, who showed us what a little thing life is. There it took a superhuman effort to remain alive. Typhus and debilitation – well, yes. But I feel certain that Anne died of her sister's death. Dying is so frightfully easy for anyone left alone in a concentration camp."

CHAPTER 13

The Diary of Anne Frank

My forty-two witnesses have said what was to be said; the story is done. The trail of a child has come to light, a delicate track – and the shadow of the blackest nightmare.

"I see it all now as though from a great distance," Henk said in conclusion, "and I see it as if through a mist. But the mist, too, is already far away. It is of the strangest colour. Not dark, not that, but the colour cannot be described."

Miep said:

"We never guessed that it would all come back to us, so powerfully and so immediately. When I saw myself running on to the stage and heard myself crying, 'Have you heard? The invasion has begun! The invasion has begun!' and when they all embraced one another in sheer joy, I suddenly found myself gripping my seat in the theatre and the hope, *all* the hope I had felt then, came back to me – until I told myself: 'Why, you're mad. It's all over now.'

"I looked upon the play as a story out of the lives of perfect strangers, and seeing it in those terms, I thought very well of it. Please understand me aright: I lived through it all then, to the very end, and one does not have the strength to do so more than once. At the time I was shaken, and at the time I wept. But when I see it all again now, I cannot weep.

"There it unrolls before me, three acts, scene upon scene, and I look up and ask myself: 'Is that you? But you didn't have a hat on when you came in that time. After all, you were coming right from the office.' That is why I did not have to feel it again and weep again. Seeing the play was only a partial going back for me, and my life went on."

Anne's papers are preserved in a sheet-metal box, and the box is in an old green office safe in Amsterdam. I have seen it. In the box lies the diary with the red checked cover in which Anne began to write, and the office account books into which the diary overflowed, and in between lies a stack of 312 tissue-thin sheets of paper of various colours, all covered with Anne's close, neatly flowing handwriting.

In addition to the diary Anne wrote more than a dozen stories, some fine-spun and dreamily melancholy, others so precise in their descriptions that they resemble reportage. But neither dreaminess nor delight in reporting was the impulse behind her writing. Always she was impelled by an incredible sense of responsibility for every little and big thing in this world.

The beginning of a novel was also found among her papers. It was to be entitled *Cady's Life*, and opens with a car accident and the slow convalescence of the girl Cady. From a few scenes she had sketched out, from completed parts, and from an outline found among her diary entries, it is apparent that Anne intended to weave her own fate into this novel, or the fate of Lies as she had dreamed it one night. But the story was to be told from outside, from the point of view of freedom. Cady was to live in freedom. There is a mention of Mary, her friend, a Jewish girl, who is to be taken away by the Nazis. But what Mary's fate specifically was to be, the fragments do not make clear.

Concerning the beginning of this novel, Anne had written:

I have many ideas, and am busy assembling them. But since I have no paper, I shall have to start writing from the back.

And she took her account-book diary, the one she was currently using, which was to be her last, turned it around, and began *Cady's Life* in the same notebook. Thus diary and novel ran towards one another in the notebook. Some day they would meet, collide somewhere in the middle of the book.

In her last diary entry Anne wrote:

Dear Kitty,
'Little bundle of contradictions.' That's how I ended my last letter and that's how I'm going to begin this one. 'A little bundle of contradictions,' can you tell me exactly what it is? What does contradiction mean? Like so many words, it can mean two things, contradiction from without and contradiction from within.

And the last lines of her novel read:

Cady had a premonition that Mary would no longer be there, and sure enough, when she came to the house, the door was bolted. Then Cady was overcome by a terrible sense of discouragement. Who knows where she is now... she thought. Immediately she turned around and went home, hurried to her room and locked the door. Still in her coat, she dropped on to the sofa, and her thoughts were with Mary.

Why had they taken Mary, while she remained behind? Why must Mary suffer such a terrible fate – while she could go on enjoying things? Was there a difference between them? Was she any better than Mary? Had they not been alike, and what crime had Mary committed? It was the most fearful of injustices, and suddenly she saw Mary's small figure before her, locked in a cell, clothed in rags, with hollow, emaciated face...

Cady's strength gave out. She fell to her knees and cried, cried... And she saw before her a band of rough armed men and heard the doors slamming, the children weeping, and among them, helpless and alone, Mary, who was exactly like herself. Mary...

That is the end of the fragmentary novel.

Who knows what would have happened if her novel and her diary had some day collided in the middle of the notebook? That point was not reached, for a small number of pages remained blank between these two last entries.

Elli and Miep found Anne's papers during the week after the police raid on the Prinsengracht hide-out.

Miep says:

"It was terrible, when I went up there. Not a soul in the place. The rooms suddenly looked so big. Everything had been turned upside down and rummaged through. On the floor lay clothes, papers, letters and school notebooks. Anne's little wrap hung from a hook on the wall. I took it with me. And among the papers on the floor lay a notebook with a checked red cover. I picked it up, looked at the pages and recognised Anne's handwriting."

Elli says, weeping:

"The table was still set; there were plates, cups, and spoons, but the plates empty, and I was so frightened I scarcely dared to take a step. I, too, saw the papers on the floor, and I said to Miep:

"'Look, Miep, there is Anne's handwriting, too.'

"We sat down on the floor and leafed through all the papers. They were all Anne's, the notebooks and the coloured duplicate paper from the office, too. We gathered them up and took them down with us. Downstairs, in the main office, we locked up all of it.

"A few days later M came into the office, M who now had the keys of the building. He said to me: 'I found some more stuff upstairs.'

"What he gave me was more of Anne's papers, and I thought: You would be the one to give these to me! But I took them and put them away with the others, and shut the locker again."

In regard to one point Elli may be mistaken. Miep did not notice a set table, and Mr Frank commented that the table would not have been set, since it was only half past ten when the police came, and by then the breakfast things had always been cleared and the table would not yet have been set for lunch. But Elli insists:

"I did see them, all eight plates, right around the table. Only the plates were empty…"

The two women kept Anne's papers until Mr Frank returned after the war. He came via Odessa and Marseilles. *Monoway* was the name of the ship that brought the rescued concentration-camp inmates from Odessa to Marseilles. It flew the New Zealand flag. A ship had to come from New Zealand so that a few survivors from Europe could return home to Europe.

Miep and Elli did not read Anne's papers at the time, they told me. They only leafed through the notebooks, and when they identified them as Anne's, they locked them up. Thus her voice was preserved out of the millions that were silenced, this voice no louder than a child's whisper. It tells how those millions lived, spoke, ate, and slept, and it has outlasted the shouts of the murderers and has soared above the voices of time.

Anne Frank Ambassadors' training day

The Anne Frank Trust UK

The Anne Frank Trust was set up in 1990 by family and friends of Otto Frank to carry out his wish to see an educational organisation in Britain in his daughter's memory. The Trust is a registered charity whose mission is to draw on the life and diary of Anne Frank to challenge prejudice and reduce hatred, and encourage people to embrace positive attitudes, responsibility and respect for others.

The Anne Frank Trust educates over 40,000 young people a year through exhibitions and educational programmes in schools, prisons and community settings, targeting areas of deprivation and division. The Trust also trains young Anne Frank Ambassadors, runs national campaigns and encourages people to sign up to the Anne Frank Declaration.

For more information about the Anne Frank Trust and its work and how you can support it see

www.annefrank.org.uk

The Anne Frank Trust UK

Registered charity number 1003279 Scottish charity number SC040488

The Anne Frank House

Anne Frank's life story helps to make the fate of millions of victims of the Holocaust more personal and comprehensible to us. It is a story that begins with prejudice and pre-conceptions: problems that still lead to anti-Semitism and other forms of discrimination, exclusion and persecution in all parts of the world today.

Mission

Through the efforts of Otto Frank and a group of dedicated benefactors, on 3 May 1957 the Anne Frank House was set up as a charitable foundation: an independent, non-profit organisation dedicated to the preservation and opening to the public of Anne Frank's hiding place, and to bringing the life story of Anne Frank to the attention of as many people as possible worldwide.

The Anne Frank House also develops educational programmes and products based on Anne Frank's life story, with the aim of raising young people's awareness of the dangers of anti-Semitism, racism and discrimination and the importance of freedom, equal rights and democracy.

Partners

The Anne Frank House works together with key partner organisations in the United Kingdom, Germany, the United States of America, Austria and Argentina. These support the Anne Frank House in disseminating the life story of Anne Frank. The Anne Frank House also works together with related organisations in many other countries.

anne frank
house